STREETWISE®

BUSINESS LETTERS

STREETWISE®

BUSINESS LETTERS

2,500 Professionally-
Written Letters That
Will Bring Success
to Your Business

by John Woods

Adams Media Corporation
Avon, Massachusetts

A Streetwise® Publication.
Streetwise® is a registered trademark of Adams Media Corporation.

Published by Adams Media Corporation
57 Littlefield Street, Avon, MA 02322. U.S.A.
adamsmedia.com

ISBN: 1-58062-133-3

Printed in the United States of America.

J   I   H   G   F   E   D

Library of Congress Cataloging-in-Publication Data
Woods, John A.
Streetwise business letters / John Woods.
p.   cm.
Includes index.
ISBN 1-58062-133-3
1. Commercial Correspondence. I. Title.
HF5726.W75   1999
651.7'5–dc21   99-26116
CIP

This book was developed for Adams Media Corporation by CWL Publishing Enterprises, John Woods,
President, 3010 Irvington Way, Madison, WI 53713, www.execpc.com/cwlpubent.

This publication is designed to provide accurate and authoritative information with regard to the subject matter covered. It is sold with the understanding that the publisher is not engaged in rendering legal, accounting, or other professional advice. If legal advice or other expert assistance is required, the services of a competent professional person should be sought.
— From a *Declaration of Principles* jointly adopted by a Committee of the American Bar Association and a Committee of Publishers and Associations

Cover illustration by Eric Mueller.

Visit our exciting small business Web site at businesstown.com

Table of Contents

Contents

IV. Chapter Four: Public Relations & Publicity 239

V. Chapter Five: Customer Service 261

A. Complaints 263

Contents

VII. Chapter Seven: Accounting & Finance 353

Introduction

You now hold in your hands the most comprehensive guide to business letters available. No other book, disc, or CD-ROM has as many examples, covers as many situations, and saves you as much time as *Streetwise Business Letters*.

As a professional, you probably have chosen this book to accomplish two major goals. Number one is to save time. And since time is money, you've probably realized that valuable asset is better spent on developing marketing plans, cutting costs, and finding new customers than in pondering the finer points between "insure" and "ensure."

Number two is to communicate effectively and in a professional manner. Let's face it, there's no point in saving time by using prewritten business letters if they're not top-notch.

Well, not to worry. *Streetwise Business Letters* will save you time and money and present your business in the most professional manner possible. For starters, you can't find as many example letters anywhere else. The book portion of this package provides 350 samples from some of the most common, everyday business situations you'll face. And if you want to find one of these letters on the enclosed CD-ROM, simply insert the disk, click on Open a Master Document and follow the steps outlined at the bottom of the letter you have chosen from the book. Then, if you encounter special situations, you'll find over 2,000 more letters on the enclosed CD-ROM. You simply can't beat that.

You can accomplish your first goal of saving money immediately. If you use just *one* letter, you'll probably save an hour of your valuable time right off the bat. This hour alone is more than worth the purchase price. And if you continue to use this resource throughout the life of your business, you'll save *countless* hours and dollars!

Your second goal of communicating in an effective and professional manner has already been accomplished: you've chosen this book. Each letter was written by a business professional and author of several business books.

So whether you want to send out formal business correspondence or a simple thank-you note, *Streetwise Business Letters* has the right letter, written in a professional manner, ready for you.

Sales Letters

If you don't have sales, you have nothing. Businesses fail because of lack of sales. That's it. So, obviously a good portion of this book has been devoted to sales letters. Most are formatted to outside sources, but some are geared toward your internal sales force. These letters cover motivation, managing change, providing good and bad news, and performance. The letters to outside customers cover everything from accompanying a catalog to requesting a meeting to asking for a referral and more. But whatever the purpose of a sales letter, or any other letter for that matter, there are several key points you want to keep in mind: the Seven Cs.

1. Be clear. This is the cornerstone of effective communication and requires considerable effort on the writer's part. It includes writing to the reader's level of understanding, but not down to the reader. It means using language, words, and phrases that the reader understands, while avoiding all jargon and unfamiliar words and phrases. It involves coherently and logically ordering thoughts and ideas and structuring paragraphs so that each idea has its own place in the letter. Good narratives are designed to make the desired impact. Remember, it is the writer's obligation to clearly communicate so that the reader can understand, not the other way around.

2. Be complete. Good writing includes all the information necessary to make the point and promote whatever action the letter requests. The data must be designed with a purpose in mind. Random details and thoughts, however colorful and interesting, only confuse the reader if they are not relevant to the issues being raised. Stay on track and make sure you have provided the reader with enough information to encourage the action you seek.

3. Be concise. "Brevity is the soul of wit," William Shakespeare once wrote. Plainly put, keep letters short and to the point. Do not pad your communication if the padding does not address the main point or contribute to the letter's goal. Readers will be annoyed, not impressed, by verbiage that obstructs rather than expedites the communication process.

4. Be concrete. Use numbers, ratios, and facts whenever they are available rather than prose that attempts to paraphrase those particulars. If you are talking about a recent order that has failed to arrive, identify the shipping code and contents of that order. This will help speed the process and clarify the communication's intent.

5. Be constructive. Words and phrases that set a positive tone or cast recipients' actions (or inactions) in the most positive light possible receive a better response, and thus more effectively accomplish their goal. By giving the benefit of the doubt, you are more likely to get the reader on your side. It doesn't always work, but it's worth the effort.

6. Be conversational. The bane of business communication tends to be the BusinessSpeak in which much of it is written. Writing that is informal and conversational will be more easily understood and better received. You cannot afford to bypass the letter's other obligations and restrictions, but writing in a casual style will result in more effective communications.

7. Be correct. Despite mastery of these other steps, letter writers cannot be effective if they ignore accuracy. This includes errors in structure, spelling, grammar, fact, and opinion. Make use of whatever spelling and grammar checking tools your word processor may have, and proofread drafts and finished copies rigorously. When possible, have another person proofread your letters. We all make mistakes, but even a tiny one creeping into your final text undermines your credibility as a communicator and casts a shadow over every other element of your message.

Is there a flip side to all of this? Are there Seven Deadly Sins of Writing? Just turn the Seven Cs around and you'll have those sins.

Accompanying a catalog

[DATE]

[Name]
[Company]
[Address]
[City, State ZIP]

Dear [   ]:

When your mother calls, you're on your motorcycle. And well you should be. Any cycling enthusiast knows after-work and weekend hours are prime times for riding.

Mother may already have gone to bed by the time you come in. But we haven't. Our catalog order lines are open 24 hours a day, seven days a week. That means you can order the parts you need at times when you're not riding.

You'll be pleased with [company]'s products as well as our service. [We feature original equipment manufacturer parts for most bikes made between 1975 and the present.] And we deliver in two to three business days—so you can get back out riding.

Bottom line is, your satisfaction is guaranteed. If you're not happy with any part of your experience with [company], just let us know. We'll happily take back any item you've purchased and refund your money.

Next time you take a break from riding, give us a call!

Sincerely,

[Name]
[Title]

- **Show how catalog shopping fits your prospect's lifestyle.**

- **State any special warranties or guarantees in the letter as well as in the catalog.**

Path on CD-ROM: Marketing/Sales→Sales→Accompanying a catalog→Accompanying a catalog—example 1

Accompanying a renewal notice

[DATE]

[Name]
[Company]
[Address]
[City, State ZIP]

Dear [   ]:

Thank you for [insuring] your [item] with [company]. The end of [your policy] year is nearing and I am enclosing renewal papers for your review.

Please look over the [declarations page, policy, and other endorsements]. If you have any questions, please call me right away. To renew, please [send a check in the amount highlighted on page [number] to me] in the enclosed self-addressed envelope.

[When you purchased your [company] insurance, you also purchased the excellent service of more than [number] agents and [number] [company] employees.] Keep in mind that we also offer [other insurance types]. I'd be happy to discuss any of these with you.

Thanks again for allowing me to handle your [insurance] needs. I appreciate your confidence.

Sincerely,

[Name]
[Title]

- **Provide the right paper work.**

- **Make the process of renewing as easy as possible.**

Path on CD-ROM: Marketing/Sales→Sales→Accompanying renewal notice→Accompanying renewal notice—example 1

Adding a "bigwig" to a prospect tour

[DATE]

[Name]
[Company]
[Address]
[City, State ZIP]

Dear [   ]:

Everyone here at [company] is pleased that you are coming to tour our site. In fact, our president/CEO, [name], was so pleased to hear you would be visiting that he has said he'll personally lead your tour.

It'll be my pleasure to introduce you to [him/her] personally. As we have already discussed, please come to [place] at [time and date]. We'll go from there.

If you have any questions before then, please don't hesitate to call me. [president's last name] and I are looking forward to showing you our quality assurance efforts.

Sincerely,

[Name]
[Title]

- **Make the prospect feel important because a "bigwig" wants to personally lead his or her tour of the site.**

- **Re-confirm the time and date of the tour.**

Path on CD-ROM: Marketing/Sales→Sales→Adding bigwig to prospect tour→Adding bigwig to prospect tour—example 1

Announcing a sales contest

INTEROFFICE MEMORANDUM

TO: [   ]
FROM: [   ]
DATE: [   ]
SUBJECT: [Sell your way to a getaway]

Are you ready for a [quiet weekend in the country]?

We hope so as we're about to launch [Shoes Unlimited's Country Inn Getaway Contest].

Every sales person on the team is eligible to win this all-expenses-paid getaway. The promotion begins [Jan. 2 and ends March 2]. To win a getaway, you must sign up [six new stores for delivery of our lines].

Since [Shoes Unlimited has recently started offering Web-based order tracking, many stores have been inquiring about signing up with us]. With these leads and the ones you generate yourself, you're on the way to [the country]!

Here's how the weekend will go. [You will receive a voucher for a luxury rental car, another for two nights at The Oakland Inn, Small Town, Pa., and $500 cash for food and incidentals. You and your guest will drive to the inn, enjoy the finest country hospitality, and relax in the quiet charm of the area.]

We'll kick off this contest at next week's sales meeting. Think relaxing, all-expenses-paid weekend!

- **Use a sentence that encourages the whole sales force to reach for this prize.**

- **Show your expectation of success.**

Path on CD-ROM: Marketing/Sales→Sales→Announcing a sales contest→Announcing a sales contest—example 1

Announcing an ad campaign to sales staff

INTEROFFICE MEMORANDUM

TO: [   ]
FROM: [Sales manager]
DATE: [   ]
SUBJECT: [Summer ad campaign should generate leads]

[Sail away with colorful clothes from Fitting Fashions!]

This is the theme of the new ad campaign that will be launched [June 5]. The advertising will be taking out several full-page newspaper ads, plus mailing catalogs to area residents. As the ads and catalogs go out, we will post them in the break room for your reference.

Advertising expects the campaign will generate a lot of extra sales. Happy selling!

- **Show a sense of the creative in the ad campaign.**

- **Explain how sales reps can see the ads.**

Path on CD-ROM: Marketing/Sales→Sales→Announcing ad campaign to sales staff→Announcing ad campaign to sales staff—example 1

Announcing a change in sales policy

INTEROFFICE MEMORANDUM

TO: [All sales staffers]
FROM: [Sales manager]
DATE: [   ]
SUBJECT: [Sales policy change]

Starting [July 5], there will be an extra charge of [$50] for all next-day deliveries from [Warehouse Equipment]. This is due to an increase in the charges of our delivery vendor for rush deliveries. We have considered changing to a cheaper delivery service, but have not found one of equal reliability.

Obviously the extra charge is not a selling point, but it does underscore [Warehouse Equipment's] commitment to delivering your order on time.

At [Warehouse you can get used but good office equipment for a truly affordable price.] We are committed to providing value and the best customer service in town.

We could cut corners by using a less reliable delivery system. But we prefer to be known for providing value and being on time.

When you make your sales presentations, do not be afraid to discuss this new charge. Explain that it is a benefit to work with a company committed to on-time delivery.

- **Explain the reasons for the change.**

- **Show how the change can be sold as a benefit to customers.**

Path on CD-ROM: Marketing/Sales→Sales→Announcing change in sales policy→Announcing change in sales policy—example 1

Announcing a new catalog

[DATE]

[Name]
[Company]
[Address]
[City, State ZIP]

Dear [   ]:

Just the [part] you want. On the day you want it. That's the [company] catalog difference.

Using our new [title] catalog, you'll be able to order from our new and extensive list of [hard-to-find parts] for [professional equipment]. When you place an order, just tell us how fast you want it—we have delivery options to fit every need.

Our catalog customer care representatives are standing by 24 hours a day, seven days a week, ready to take your order. Just call [800 number] to get the part you want when you want it.

Thanks in advance for your order.

Sincerely,

[Name]
[Title]

- **Highlight the professional nature of the catalog.**

- **Show the benefits of ordering.**

Path on CD-ROM: Marketing/Sales→Sales→Announcing new catalog→Announcing new catalog—example 1

Announcing new products

[DATE]

[Name]
[Company]
[Address]
[City, State ZIP]

Dear [   ]:

[Like-New Piano Restoration Services] is pleased to announce it will now be able to offer products from the [In Tune with Pianos] catalog.

As a licensed distributor of these products, [Like New Piano] will be able to get you rush delivery for the price of regular delivery on any products we order for you through the catalog. The products offered include [top-quality replacement keys and pedals, springs and music holders, as well as music lamps and metronomes].

You will love being able to get these great [piano parts and accessories from the same group that has provided you with expert tuning and repair services for years]. I am enclosing a copy of the most recent [In Tune] catalog. Remember, if you wish to order anything, we can get you rush delivery for the price of regular.

Thank you for your continued business. We look forward to providing you with this new offering.

Sincerely,

[Name]
[Title]

- **Elaborate on the new product or service offered.**

- **Show the benefit of the new offering.**

Path on CD-ROM: Marketing/Sales→Sales→Announcing new products→Announcing new products—example 1

Announcing a price decrease

[DATE]

[Name]
[Company]
[Address]
[City, State ZIP]

Dear [   ]:

How'd you like to get the same high-quality produce you always have—for less? Now, you can, with [Fresh from the Farm Produce].

How can we afford to offer the same outstanding organic fruits and vegetables for new, lower prices? [This time it's our commitment to efficient energy use that's making things happen.]

[Last year we invested in a special super-saving irrigation system. This year, the savings from that purchase have paid back our loan, plus given us additional savings that allow the price decrease!]

We know you enjoy getting the safest, tastiest produce around. Now you can get it at an even better price. Stop by [Fresh from the Farm Produce] soon.

Sincerely,

[Name]
[Title]

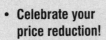

- **Celebrate your price reduction!**

- **Explain how the reduction was possible.**

Path on CD-ROM: Marketing/Sales→Sales→Announcing price decrease→Announcing price decrease—example 1

Announcing a price increase

[DATE]

[Name]
[Company]
[Address]
[City, State ZIP]

Dear [   ]:

[Electric Lines Inc.] wants you to be satisfied with your [electric service. In order to ensure service during heavy storms, we have recently installed two new devices at our area substations that will help us bring your power back more quickly when lightning strikes occur.]

The investment necessary to provide this additional protection forces us to increase our prices by [8 percent starting June 1]. This price increase has been approved by our regulating governmental agency. You will be receiving a brochure outlining our new prices.

Thank you for your understanding. We want only to provide the utmost in service.

Sincerely,

[Name]
[Title]

- **Show the benefit customers will get from some recent company investment.**

- **Detail the price increase and when it will start.**

Path on CD-ROM: Marketing/Sales→Sales→Announcing a price increase→Announcing a price increase—example 1

Approaching new contact at current client company

[DATE]

[Name]
[Company]
[Address]
[City, State ZIP]

Dear [   ]:

New blood is the lifeblood of great organizations such as [prospect company]. I'm looking forward to starting to work with you on new proposals and carrying through on existing projects.

As you might have been briefed, [predecessor] and I have been working on [project] and [project]. These efforts should [outcome]. In addition, I would like to sit down with you to talk about the new ideas you have and ways my company and I can help you meet your goals. Please feel free to ask me questions or for detailed information on current or future projects.

It's been a pleasure having so many successful ventures with [predecessor], and I'm equally enthusiastic about working with you. I'll call next week to set up a time to meet.

Sincerely,

[Name]
[Title]

- Do not assume the new person will continue on the same path as his or her predecessor.

- Show enthusiasm for the past work and successes as well as for the future.

Path on CD-ROM: Marketing/Sales→Sales→Approaching new contact at current client company→Approaching new contact at current client company—example 1

Approaching new management after old management rejection

[DATE]

[Name]
[Company]
[Address]
[City, State ZIP]

Dear [   ]:

Here's the straight-up story: you could easily make additional revenues for your company by [selling reprints of your publication's articles].

Maybe previous management had its reasons for not [offering reprints], but I just couldn't figure them out. With [company] managing your reprint orders, a conservative estimate puts sales at [amount]. Our phone marketing staff is polished and professional; they'll be instructed to treat your contacts and sources with the utmost respect. No one will be forced to buy.

Even so, you stand to make money now by signing on with [company]. I'll call you [when] to see if you're ready to rectify this situation to the benefit of your organization.

Sincerely,

[Name]
[Title]

- **Call your statements "frank" as an attention-getter.**

- **Explain the reasons the new management should buy from you, even though past management was inactive.**

Path on CD-ROM: Marketing/Sales→Sales→Approaching new management after rejection→Approaching new management after rejection—example 1

Asking for a testimonial letter

[DATE]

[Name]
[Title]
[Company]
[Address]
[City, State ZIP]

Dear [   ]:

Your presentation was the highlight of the whole conference! We felt honored to be able to do the [lighting and sound] for you. We felt we were able to provide a [dramatic environment that really enhanced your presence.]

Do you agree? If so, would you consider writing us a short letter of recommendation that we could use when we tell others about our services?

Thank you for considering this. We look forward to serving your needs again.

Sincerely,

[Name]
[Title]

- State what you think was good about your product or service and ask the customer to agree.

- Be clear that the testimonial, if given, would be used in your marketing efforts.

Path on CD-ROM: Marketing/Sales→Sales→Asking for a testimonial letter→Asking for a testimonial letter—example 1

Avoiding a business sales pitch

[DATE]

[Name]
[Company]
[Address]
[City, State ZIP]

Dear [   ]:

Thank you very much for writing to tell me about [product] and your company. I was very impressed by your excellent knowledge of your line.

As you know, I've been doing business with [name] for [number] years. While I'm intrigued with [some of the products in your line], I really feel that loyalty is important and that I need to honor the longtime healthy relationship I've built with [name]. I know you can understand how this is at the basis of my decision not to place an order with you at this time.

Thank you again for telling me about [company].

Sincerely,

[Name]
[Title]

- **Send a letter like this if you want to promote business goodwill, even when you are not buying the product.**

- **Discourage the sales person from following up.**

Path on CD-ROM: Marketing/Sales→Sales→Avoiding business sales pitch→Avoiding business sales pitch—example 10

Closing to overcome "business is bad now" objection

[DATE]

[Name]
[Company]
[Address]
[City, State ZIP]

Dear [   ]:

When I heard that your great company was experiencing a sales slow down, I talked to my supervisor about how [company] might be able to help.

Here are the great suggestions he had to offer:

[1. We'll deliver 200 products from our new catalog immediately. Since your inventory hasn't been turning over, this will give you new items to merchandise.]

[2. I'll personally come by and give your clerks an in-store creative displays seminar, helping to boost morale and get the new products set out.]

[3. We'll extend credit for 30 days, so you won't have to pay us until you've sold many of them, and have the money in hand!]

You can't lose! I'll call you in a couple of days to set up a date for the products' delivery.

Sincerely,

[Name]
[Title]

- **Make the prospect feel important by talking to your boss.**

- **Show how buying your product will actually boost the prospect's sluggish sales.**

Path on CD-ROM: Marketing/Sales→Sales→Closing to overcome business bad now→Closing to overcome business bad now—example 1

Closing to overcome "customers don't ask for your product" objection

[DATE]

[Name]
[Company]
[Address]
[City, State ZIP]

Dear [   ]:

When companies hire employees, they know they need to compile a team of people with a variety of skills and interests—a player skilled in each of the functions needed to run the company.

In much the same way, stores need to choose their stock to provide "something for everyone." While you have let me know that customers rarely ask for [company] [products], I am confident that if you had them on your shelves, they would not only consistently turn over, but also bring back a new kind of customer that used to shop your store just once.

So just as you've put together employees with varied skills, you'll be pleased when you add [company] [product] to your product variety. I'll stop by in a few days to show you some samples and some research on how our products have helped other retailers grow their customer base.

Sincerely,

[Name]
[Title]

- **Show the benefits of stocking the "rarely requested" product.**

- **Offer to show the product, and provide additional supporting material.**

Path on CD-ROM: Marketing/Sales→Sales→Closing to overcome customers don't ask for product→Closing to overcome customers don't ask for product—example 1

Closing to overcome high price objection

[DATE]

[Name]
[Company]
[Address]
[City, State ZIP]

Dear [   ]:

Diamonds are forever. Every woman knows it, and many dream of that perfect diamond anniversary ring. It's even more special if it comes in a [company] box.

That little box seems to cost more. But in reality, when you buy from [company] you're getting more than extra brownie points with your loved one. You're getting a guarantee of the highest quality materials and workmanship. You're getting our promise of the highest level of customer service. And, you're getting exclusive designs that could only come out of our workshop.

Listen to some things our clients say:

["My wife loved her anniversary band from [company]. She was excited as soon as she saw the little black box."]

["I love the peace of mind I get buying from a jeweler that's so committed to quality and service."]

["It's for my wife, but I think it's gorgeous, too. [company] designs are truly out of this world."]

When you buy from [company], you will satisfy yourself and your loved one.

Sincerely,

[Name]
[Title]

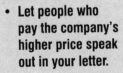

- Let people who pay the company's higher price speak out in your letter.

- Show how the quality and service are worth the extra money.

Path on CD-ROM: Marketing/Sales→Sales→Closing to overcome high price objection→Closing to overcome high price objection—example 1

Closing to overcome "I always do business with someone else" objection

[DATE]

[Name]
[Company]
[Address]
[City, State ZIP]

Dear [   ]:

As a salesman, I have to appreciate customer loyalty. I respect your wanting to continue to buy from [competitor].

Indeed, I'm not trying to diminish your business relationship with [competitor]. Rather, I'm trying to augment it.

As you know, our [line] line has been selling like hot cakes at other retail establishments. Because [competitor] doesn't offer these products, you could very safely order these from [company] and still maintain a loyal relationship with [competitor].

No one would fault you for wanting to develop your line, especially considering the increasing competition in your industry. [In particular, I am thinking of the new store that opened up just six miles from your main location.]

Be loyal to [competitor] by continuing to buy from them. Be loyal to yourself by adding our [line] to your offerings. The first time you buy, we'll throw in a 10 percent discount and free delivery.

I'll call you next week to take your order.

Sincerely,

[Name]
[Title]

- **Show respect for loyalty.**

- **Mention how adding your products can increase the prospect's competitiveness.**

Path on CD-ROM: Marketing/Sales→Sales→Closing to overcome I always do business with someone else→Closing to overcome I always do business with someone else—example 1

Closing to overcome "I'm happy with what I've got" objection

[DATE]

[Name]
[Company]
[Address]
[City, State ZIP]

Dear [   ]:

Innovation is the way of the marketplace. Sometimes these innovations, such as automobiles, practically wipe out previous industries, like the railroad.

While I don't necessarily mean to suggest that [prospect] would completely lose its ability to compete because it didn't purchase [product], I do think that not buying would dull [prospect]'s competitive edge.

I also am aware that [prospect]'s chief competitor, [competitor], has been moving forward with a similar product from another supplier. The [product] has been saving them so much staff time that they've been able to reassign several employees to research new product lines and other strategies for gaining competitive advantage.

I know you like your current product. But let me show you how [company]'s [product] can really make a competitive difference for you. I'll call you next week about setting up a demonstration.

Sincerely,

[Name]
[Title]

- **Show how the product would help the prospect keep its competitive edge.**

- **If you have data on a competitor's use of the product, use it as strong incentive.**

Path on CD-ROM: Marketing/Sales→Sales→Closing to overcome I'm happy with what I've got→Closing to overcome I'm happy with what I've got—example 1

Closing to overcome "It's new" objection

[DATE]

[Name]
[Company]
[Address]
[City, State ZIP]

Dear [   ]:

My father was famous for only eating chocolate ice cream. "Is there any other kind?" he used to say.

Then, when traveling in Spain, a colleague challenged him to step out of the box and try "turron" flavor, a Spanish specialty. Since another of my father's favorite sayings is, "When in Rome, do as the Romans," he had to try it.

And, you know what? He liked it. "I don't know why I never tried another flavor before!"

Now, my father didn't earn any more money because he tried a new flavor of ice cream. But you and your company stand to benefit greatly for trying [product] from [company].

In particular, you'll experience the benefits of:

[benefit]
[benefit]
[benefit]
[benefit]

I know if you try [company]'s [product], we'll develop a long-term business relationship. You'll be saying, "I don't know why I never tried this before!"

I'll call you next week to see if you're ready for something new.

Sincerely,

[Name]
[Title]

- **Show the potential benefits of trying something new.**

- **Use a personal anecdote to help make the point in a friendly way.**

Path on CD-ROM: Marketing/Sales→Sales→Closing to overcome it's new objection→Closing to overcome it's new objection—example 1

Closing to overcome "low price must mean low quality" objection

[DATE]

[Name]
[Company]
[Address]
[City, State ZIP]

Dear [   ]:

Some of my friends refuse to shop discounted clothing retailers. I like to go there and buy name-brand fashions for half the price.

Why won't my friends take advantage of the savings? They are sure that the discounted stores sell lesser quality goods. In fact, they sell only first-rate goods that are leftovers from the even lots the department stores buy.

Moral of the story? A lower price doesn't necessarily mean lower quality.

From our discussions, I'm quite sure that [prospect company] will realize a [amount] savings this year if you choose to buy [product] from [company]. Our [products], while less expensive, are every bit as high quality as those you currently purchase.

The choice is yours—join me in getting name-brand for less. Or, spend more for the same product.

Sincerely,

[Name]
[Title]

- **Stress that the product, although less expensive, is of the same quality.**

- **Call for action by giving the prospect a clearly defined choice.**

Path on CD-ROM: Marketing/Sales→Sales→Closing to overcome low price must mean low quality objection→Closing to overcome low price must mean low quality objection—example 1

Closing to overcome the "next trip" objection

[DATE]

[Name]
[Company]
[Address]
[City, State ZIP]

Dear [   ]:

Thanks for meeting with me on [day]. I know you didn't want to talk about [products] again until my next visit to your office, but I've learned something important and I thought I should tell you.

During my trip, our prices increased [10] percent across the board. However, customers who expressed interest in buying our product in the three weeks before the increase have a special opportunity to buy at our old prices. At the quantities we've been discussing, you would save [amount].

But only until [date].

Please call us with your order and take advantage of this limited-time offer. The [date] deadline cannot be extended.

Sincerely,

[Name]
[Title]

- **Show respect for the request to think about it until the next trip.**

- **Set an absolute deadline to encourage action.**

Path on CD-ROM: Marketing/Sales→Sales→Closing to overcome the next trip objection→Closing to overcome the next trip objection—example 1

Closing to overcome "retail price too high" objection

[DATE]

[Name]
[Company]
[Address]
[City, State ZIP]

Dear [   ]:

Some people look at a glass with milk in it and call if half empty; others call it half full. It all depends on your perspective.

As you look at the selling price of our [product], you've been calling it too high sell. We urge you to take another look.

Our [products] have been selling really well in all our retail outlets. They're appealing in their own right. Every [target person] wants one. And, our higher price, in support of our higher quality, is part of what makes our products so popular.

There's no better time to try out how they sell than right before the Christmas holiday. Give your customers a chance to tell you for certain whether they see the glass as half empty or half full. We're willing to bet they'll buy more than you project.

I hope you'll be ready to look at things with a new perspective when I call you next week.

Sincerely,

[Name]
[Title]

- **Suggest a change in perspective about your product's price, stressing the quality it supports and how well it's selling already.**

- **Tie your appeal to a holiday if possible.**

Path on CD-ROM: Marketing/Sales→Sales→Closing to overcome retail price too high→Closing to overcome retail price too high—example 1

Closing to overcome the "my boss decides" objection

[DATE]

[Name]
[Company]
[Address]
[City, State ZIP]

Dear [   ]:

Would you like to make yourself and your supervisor the next pair of company heroes? Read and act on the enclosed information.

As you look it over, notice that [company] has been the leading [product] producer for the [industry] industry for the last [number] years. Our products continue to grow in popularity.

Why are we so often chosen by business leaders in your industry? Because of our high quality. Because of our on-time delivery. Because of our knowledgeable and friendly technical support staff. Because of our competitive price.

Point out these things to your supervisor as reasons to change to [company]. And, show her the articles and the survey I've enclosed. Making the change will make both of you look good.

Sincerely,

[Name]
[Title]

- **Provide supporting data to help your contact make the case to his or her superior.**

- **Gently use ego to encourage action.**

Path on CD-ROM: Marketing/Sales→Sales→Closing to overcome the my boss decides→Closing to overcome the my boss decides—example 1

Closing to overcome "think about it" objection

[DATE]

[Name]
[Company]
[Address]
[City, State ZIP]

Dear [   ]:

The old adage, "good things come to those who wait," applies in many circumstances—but not this one.

Now is the ideal time to buy [product] from [company]. Every day you wait costs you money and staff time. In addition, the special introductory offer now being offered expires [date]. [Finally, government regulations require you to have or hire professional management of this area of your operations. You can't afford to be cited for ignoring this.]

I respect customers' need to think buying decisions through. In this case, I must urge you to act. Let [company] manage your [function].

Sincerely,

[Name]
[Title]

- **Create a sense of urgency, noting problems that may occur if the prospect waits.**

- **Do not use this tactic too often, lest you be deemed untrustworthy.**

Path on CD-ROM: Marketing/Sales→Sales→Closing to overcome think about it objection→Closing to overcome think about it objection—example 1

Closing with "be first"

[DATE]

[Name]
[Company]
[Address]
[City, State ZIP]

Dear [   ]:

Remember when you were the first kid on the block to get a shiny new bicycle? It was a great feeling, pedaling and coasting on your shiny new bike while the rest of your friends lugged out their old ones. Didn't it just make you feel like doing a wheelie?

You'll feel the same way when you're the first one in your industry network to have [product]. As the popularity of this product grows, everyone will buy one. But right now you have a chance to get in on the ground floor—to have that feeling of celebrating with a wheelie because you're first.

It's been [three months] since this product was announced and interest is building rapidly. Don't wait. Be ready to place an order when I call next week.

Sincerely,

[Name]
[Title]

- **Appeal to the prospect's emotional need to be "first."**

- **Create urgency with some kind of deadline.**

Path on CD-ROM: Marketing/Sales→Sales→Closing with be first→Closing with be first—example 1

Closing with "before and after"

[DATE]

[Name]
[Company]
[Address]
[City, State ZIP]

Dear [   ]:

Can you believe it is still just regular phone-line Web access?

Your research staff couldn't believe the speed they could get when surfing the Internet after our computer jockeys "souped up" a demonstration computer in your office. Sites that once took a minute to load showed up colorful and clear in 20 seconds. Searches that took two minutes to complete punched out the answers in half a minute! Think of the time that will save them—and you.

I'd like to show you what your staff has already seen. There's definitely a reason that they are recommending you hire [company] to work on your computers. I'll call you next week to set up a time for me to personally show you what a "souped up" system can do.

Sincerely,

[Name]
[Title]

- **Use a "before" and "after" to demonstrate the reason for buying your product or service.**

- **Offer a personal demonstration to the decision maker.**

Path on CD-ROM: Marketing/Sales→Sales→Closing with before and after→Closing with before and after—example 1

Closing with customization offer

[DATE]

[Name]
[Company]
[Address]
[City, State ZIP]

Dear [   ]:

Thank you so much for talking with me on the phone last week. I have been thinking about your needs for a [product or service].

Although we had talked about providing you with one of our standard solutions, I have come to believe that a custom [product or service] would be much better for your company for the following reasons:

1. [reason]
2. [reason]
3. [reason]

Customization of the system means your staff will have more time to attend to other tasks. In less than a year, this time savings is very likely to completely set off the costs of a custom system.

That's what several of our clients that have purchased custom systems tell us. They would be glad to talk to you, too. I am enclosing a list of several people you can feel free to contact.

I'll give you a call next week to see if you agree that a custom solution is for you.

Sincerely,

[Name]
[Title]

- **Explain how the extra cost of a custom system can be offset.**

- **Consider providing references.**

Path on CD-ROM: Marketing/Sales→Sales→Closing with customization offer→Closing with customization offer—example 1

Closing with points of agreement

[DATE]

[Name]
[Company]
[Address]
[City, State ZIP]

Dear [   ]:

After our really productive meeting last week, I'm even more enthusiastic than ever about working with you. As we discussed, [company] will help you:

1. [task]

2. [task]

3. [task]

4. [task]

5. [task]

When we have completed our efforts, your company will [benefit to be experienced]. Thanks for this opportunity to confirm our discussion and action plan. I'll call you in a few days to set up the timetable on which to proceed.

Sincerely,

[Name]
[Title]

- **Enumerate the points agreed upon in the last meeting or discussion.**

- **Ask for confirmation of the enumerated points.**

Path on CD-ROM: Marketing/Sales→Sales→Closing with points of agreement→Closing with points of agreement—example 1

Closing with a special introductory offer

[DATE]

[Name]
[Company]
[Address]
[City, State ZIP]

Dear [   ]:

I think you would make a good decision in doing business with us at any time. But if you become a new [company] client before [deadline], you'll be able to take advantage of a special, limited-time introductory offer.

You've been thinking about it anyway. You know that [product] will give you all the benefits you want—[list benefits].

Perhaps an extra [percentage] off will be just the ticket to helping you make a good decision. That's the discount you'll get when you place your first order with [company] before the [date] deadline.

I'll call you next week about taking your order.

Sincerely,

[Name]
[Title]

- **Try this with new customers in particular.**

- **Sell the product as well as the promotion.**

Path on CD-ROM: Marketing/Sales→Sales→Closing with special introductory offer→Closing with special introductory offer—example 1

Closing with success stories

[DATE]

[Name]
[Company]
[Address]
[City, State ZIP]

Dear [   ]:

Thank you so much for talking with me on the phone last week. I was pleased to learn about your company's long- and short-term goals.

I think I mentioned on the phone that [company] has an outstanding record for helping businesses [achievement]. In a recent case, [company] helped one organization [specific measured success].

Because you work in a related industry, I am confident we could do the same thing for you.

When we meet next week I will ask you if you are interested in letting [company] help [client company] achieve success in this area.

Thanks again for your interest in [company].

Sincerely,

[Name]
[Title]

- **Use a success story to create a reason for buying.**

- **Use an example from the prospect's industry if possible.**

Path on CD-ROM: Marketing/Sales→Sales→Closing with success stories→Closing with success stories—example 1

Closing with a trial basis

[DATE]

[Name]
[Company]
[Address]
[City, State ZIP]

Dear [   ]:

Just for you! I have gotten special permission for you to try out the [product] in your office for a free [three-week] trial. On my recognition, our sales manager has even waived the usual need for a deposit.

This is a great opportunity! Now you'll be able to experience first hand the benefits of owning a [product]. Your employees will appreciate the addition to the office as well. And trying it out costs you nothing.

After [three weeks] if you just can't have me take it away, give me a call, and we'll bill you or set up a payment plan.

Thanks for your continued interest in [company]. I'll call you [day] to see when might be a good time to bring [product] by.

Sincerely,

[Name]
[Title]

- **Make the prospect feel special for getting a chance to try the product.**

- **Assume the product will sell itself during the trial period.**

Path on CD-ROM: Marketing/Sales→Sales→Closing with trial basis→Closing with trial basis—example 1

Cold call

[DATE]

[Name]
[Company]
[Address]
[City, State ZIP]

Dear [Name]:

Isn't it time you put your business on the Web?

Having a World Wide Web site isn't just for small businesses. And it isn't a luxury. It's becoming as basic as a phone listing or a business card. A site on the World Wide Web, helps put your business on the map and show that you're serious about business.

[Turnerton Associates] can build an impressive Web site for your firm complete with custom graphics and descriptions of your principle products or services and host it for [less than $1 per day]. That's right—for [less than $1 per day] for your total cost and virtually none of your time, you can have a Web site—a Web site that you can be proud of.

To learn more about [Turnerton Associate]s give us a call at [800-475-9000]—or better yet—visit our Web site at [www.turnerton.com]. You'll find hot links to other Web sites we've built for businesses just like yours.

And what's your Web site address? Call [Turnerton Associates] today and you won't have to apologize for not being on the World Wide Web any longer!

Sincerely,

[Name]
[Title]

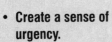

- **Create a sense of urgency.**

- **End with a call to action.**

Path on CD-ROM: Marketing/Sales→Sales→Cold call→Cold call—example 1

Confirming a sale closing meeting

[DATE]

[Name]
[Company]
[Address]
[City, State ZIP]

Dear [   ]:

Thank you so much for deciding to do business with [company].

As we have discussed, you and your company will greatly benefit from this decision. I will bring the contracts to your office for your signature at [time, date].

I look forward to welcoming you as the newest [company] customer!

Sincerely,

[Name]
[Title]

- **Reinforce that the prospect has made a good decision.**

- **Specify the time, date and place of the closing meeting.**

Path on CD-ROM: Marketing/Sales→Sales→Confirming sale closing meeting→Confirming sale closing meeting—example 1

Congratulating a sales person for a testimonial

INTEROFFICE MEMORANDUM

TO: [   ]
FROM: [   ]
DATE: [   ]
SUBJECT: [A tribute to your good work]

We just received a letter praising your good work from [ABC Shells]. President [Morgan Shelly] said you are efficient and friendly and that he enjoys doing business with you.

I know you've been working hard to make a positive impression on all your calls. It's clearly working with [ABC Shells]!

Your work is just the kind we here at [Shell Shiners] love to recognize. We are so proud of this accomplishment that [Norm] and I would like to take you out to lunch next week. When you have a chance, please stop by my office to set up a time.

Congratulations again! Keep up the good work.

- **Personalize the compliment in addition to explaining the testimonial received.**

- **Recognize the accomplishment.**

Path on CD-ROM: Marketing/Sales→Sales→Congratulating sales person for testimonial→Congratulating sales person for testimonial—example 1

Congratulating a sales person on a large sale

INTEROFFICE MEMORANDUM

TO: [   ]
FROM: [Company Sales Manager]
DATE: [   ]
SUBJECT: [Congrats on your big sale!]

Congratulations on your sale to [Ericson's]!

Looking at the records, it's the largest sale this year. I am not only pleased because it's a big sale, but also because I know how much time and effort you put in developing a relationship with [Sven]. Way to go!

With this feather in your cap, I'm sure you're feeling an added spark for future sales. As you continue on to your next big client, please let me know if there's anything I can do to help.

Again, great job!

- **Compliment the work done as well as the sale.**

- **Express an expectation for continued sales.**

Path on CD-ROM: Marketing/Sales→Sales→Congratulating sales person on large sale→Congratulating sales person on large sale—example 1

Contacting a formerly hot lead

[DATE]

[Name]
[Title]
[Company]
[Address]
[City, State ZIP]

Dear [   ]:

[Two months] ago you requested information about starting up your own [Cooking Gear] business. Our records show that we have not received your reply card requesting our official [Cooking Gear] business start-up kit.

We hope you're still interested, as running a [Cooking Gear] business is very rewarding. Just in case it's been misplaced, we've enclosed another starter kit request card. Simply fill it out and send it in. You'll get all the materials you need to get up and running within [three weeks].

Don't miss this great opportunity for a satisfying career. Send in the reply card today! Thanks for your interest.

Sincerely,

[Name]
[Title]

- **Encourage the prospect to take new action.**

- **Include a reminder of the benefits of the product or service.**

Path on CD-ROM: Marketing/Sales→Sales→Contacting formerly hot lead→Contacting formerly hot lead—example 1

Contacting a prospect whose name is unavailable

[DATE]

[Title]
[Company]
[Address]
[City, State ZIP]

Dear [title]:

I thought I was a pretty good "investigative" sales person—but with multiple calls to your office assistants, I have not been able to discern your name!

It's a little unusual writing to someone without knowing who it is exactly you're trying to reach, but I had to in this case because you need our expertise.

[I recently learned that your company had a flood in the lower level of its office. My company specializes in the restoration of buildings, documents, and everything associated with business recovery from water damage.] I've enclosed a list of satisfied clients.

I can help you clear the current recovery hurdle. Why not give me a call? Just identify yourself as the "unknown person" and I'll know just who you are.

I look forward to unveiling the mystery and to helping you immediately address your [flood recovery needs].

Sincerely,

[Name]
[Title]

- **Supply evidence of your service's benefits.**

- **Suggest that the prospect call you.**

Path on CD-ROM: Marketing/Sales→Sales→Contacting prospect whose name is unavailable→Contacting prospect whose name is unavailable—example 1

Declining to do business

[DATE]

[Name]
[Title]
[Company]
[Address]
[City, State ZIP]

Dear [   ]:

Thank you very much for your interest in doing business with [TeleDyne]. We appreciated your kind inquiry about our product lines.

Because we do not work with networks of the kind you requested, we believe we are not a good match for your [cabling] needs. Perhaps you would find the kind of expertise you seek at [Cabling Connection or TeleHook Ups].

Thanks again for your interest in [TeleDyne].

Sincerely,

[Name]
[Title]

- **Suggest that working together might not be the best move for the prospect.**

- **If possible, refer the prospect to an appropriate supplier.**

Path on CD-ROM: Marketing/Sales→Sales→Declining to do business→Declining to do business—example 1

Explaining changes in travel systems to sales people

INTEROFFICE MEMORANDUM

TO: [   ]
FROM: [   ]
DATE: [   ]
SUBJECT: Choose [hotel] when you can

The conferences department gave us a great tip—"Why not take advantage of our 'in' with [hotel] chain after the big conference we had in [city]?" they said.

Indeed, as a result of our latest event at the [hotel], the [hotel] chain has offered us a corporate-wide discount of [percent] off all stays and services.

[name] in accounting ran up the math for me. Based on these hotels' average room rate and adding in the discount, we'll save up to $[dollars] a month if we stay at these hotels and use the corporate discounts. They'll be convenient, too. We checked and there is a [hotel] hotel in all but two of our most common sales destinations.

That's over [amount] in pure profit, just for staying at a [hotel] hotel. That's equivalent to a [amount] sale!

The attached materials provide more specifics about how to take advantage of the new program. If you have specific questions, please see [name] in meetings.

This is a great change! Let's build on it!

- **Explain the reasons for the changes.**

- **Support the change with the tone of your memo.**

Path on CD-ROM: Marketing/Sales→Sales→Explaining changes in travel systems to sales people→Explaining changes in travel systems to sales people—example 1

Explaining commission plan changes to sales people

INTEROFFICE MEMORANDUM

TO: [   ]
FROM: [   ]
DATE: [   ]
SUBJECT: Changes in commission plan

Our customer base has shifted enough that we've been rethinking many ways we currently do business.

At this point, [upper management and I] agree it's time to make the [sales commission structure] reflect our new focus. The new program we're putting in place will reward [motivated sales people] more than the old one, giving you the opportunity to earn more than ever!

Instead of [paying commissions] on [old payment], we'll now pay you on [new payment]. The new way of paying will encourage sales in the area we are now targeting most heavily.

To make up for any perceived loss of potential earnings, we're also changing [change to ameliorate any sourness of the previous change].

These changes are effective now.

The attached sheet shows several examples of how the new structure will play out. As you can see, in many top sales instances, you'll earn far more than before!

Please bring any questions you have about these changes to our monthly meeting, or call me to set up a time to talk one on one.

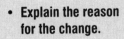

- **Explain the reason for the change.**

- **Provide examples of how the new system will work.**

Path on CD-ROM: Marketing/Sales→Sales→Explaining commission plan changes to sales people→Explaining commission plan changes to sales people—example 1

Explaining a demotion to a client

[DATE]

[Name]
[Company]
[Address]
[City, State ZIP]

Dear [   ]:

Recently I got my business card reprinted to reflect my new title: [Senior Sales Associate].

You may think, "Oh no! What happened to [name] being [sales manager]?" At first glance, the change may look like a step down; in reality it's a great change for me, for the company and for you.

I've always loved being a [sales associate]. I love to [meet with clients, discover their needs and find appropriate solutions]. As [sales manager], I was [tied to my desk too often], and I was really missing doing what I do best: [helping customers directly].

So if you see a new spring in my step, you'll know why. I'll give you a call next week to catch up and to help you find good solutions to your current needs.

Sincerely,

[Name]
[Title]

- **Explain background for the demotion.**

- **Show how the change will only benefit the client.**

Explaining a promotion to a client

[DATE]

[Name]
[Company]
[Address]
[City, State ZIP]

Dear [   ]:

It's not just that I'm getting older. I've recently completed my [degree or certificate] in [area] and have a [three-year] track record with [getting internal awards for customer service]. That's why the managers here have recently promoted me to ["Senior Sales Associate."]

Although I joke about my new job title, I take my education very seriously. It is an important part of my commitment to providing outstanding customer care. I feel really good about our working relationship. If I can ever do anything to serve you better, please let me know.

Sincerely,

[Name]
[Title]

- Explain background for promotion.

- Show how the change will only benefit the client.

Path on CD-ROM: Marketing/Sales→Sales→Explaining promotion to client→Explaining promotion to client—example 1

Explaining territory changes to sales people

INTEROFFICE MEMORANDUM

TO: [   ]
FROM: [   ]
DATE: [   ]
SUBJECT: Expanding territories

Today I offer you some room to grow.

The company has been expanding into the [area] and [area] in hopes of cultivating [new market]. It's come to the point of taking our sales efforts into these new geographic regions. I'm attaching the list of your new sales territories.

The second attached sheet lists the times I'd like to meet with each of you face to face. Please go ahead and make arrangements to travel to the home office for these meetings.

I've been talking with you about these changes for some time. Still, if you have any problems with the new set up, please tell me right away. We can discuss any issues you have at our face-to-face meeting, but I'd like to know about them in advance of getting together.

I realize this will mean extra travel and extra work for some of you. Think of it as extra sales potential. Let's bring those accounts in!

- **Explain the reasons for the changes.**

- **Set up a time to discuss territory changes with each sales person.**

Path on CD-ROM: Marketing/Sales→Sales→Explaining territory changes to sales people→Explaining territory changes to sales people—example 1

Extending a follow-up membership offer

[DATE]

[Name]
[Company]
[Address]
[City, State ZIP]

Dear [   ]:

We're so glad you're considering joining [club] as the hard-to-exercise out-doors months approach. To make joining now an even better deal, we are offering a [percentage discount off our initiation fee] to people who mention this letter when you join.

So what have you got to lose? As a member of [club], you'll enjoy meeting people, getting fit and learning new sports. Now you can do all this for less.

Stop by today and join!

Sincerely,

[Name]
[Title]

- Offer a special promotion or discount to encourage response in this follow-up letter.

- End with a call to action.

Path on CD-ROM: Marketing/Sales→Sales→Extending follow-up membership offer→Extending follow-up membership offer—example 1

Fax for a phone interview

[DATE]

1 page this fax

TO: [   ]
FROM: [   ]
RE: [   ]

Dear [   ]:

You're a tough person to reach by phone! I've tried several times with no luck. Would you call me [Wednesday at 555/555-2938]?

Sincerely,

[Name]
[Title]

- **Keep it really short.**

- **Make sure you are available at the time you specify.**

Path on CD-ROM: Marketing/Sales→Sales→Fax for phone interview→Fax for a phone interview—example 1

Faxing about preparing to make an immediate decision

[DATE]

[X] pages this fax

TO: [Territory Manager]
FROM: [General Sales Manager]
RE:

Dear [   ]:

Right before you left we finished the last interview, and we've just completed checking references on our top three candidates. As soon as you get back in the office, let's meet to make a decision about who will be the [new sales representative working the [section] section of your territory].

As we have discussed, we want this [new sales person] to [know the industry well and also have a track record of developing slow areas]. In addition, we wanted to find a personality match with the rest of your team.

Would you be sure to bring the style indicator results on the candidates to our meeting? The pages following this cover are the summary evaluations on each of the candidates we're still considering. Please review them [on your flight back tomorrow]. Can we expect you in the office by [time]?

If you have any questions, please call me right away.

Sincerely,

[Name]
[Title]

- **Explain the decision that needs to be made.**

- **Consider phoning to make sure the fax went through.**

Path on CD-ROM: Marketing/Sales→Sales→Faxing about preparing to make immediate decision→Faxing about preparing to make immediate decision—example 1

Faxing about an urgent sales issue

[DATE]

1 page this fax

TO: [   ]
FROM: [   ]
RE:

Dear [   ]:

At [3 p.m. today] I'll be onsite with my client discussing the [print] budget for next year. I promised I would bring estimates from all the [printers] we were considering. We wanted to consider you, however, we have not yet received your quote.

If you are interested in being considered for the job, would you please fax me your estimate immediately.

Thanks for your prompt response. If you want to talk with me directly, please call.

Sincerely,

[Name]
[Title]

- **Use a fax for last-minute emergencies before sales calls.**

- **Consider following up with a phone call.**

Path on CD-ROM: Marketing/Sales→Sales→Faxing about urgent sales issue→Faxing about urgent sales issue—example 1

Faxing a summary to someone who forgets what's been discussed

[DATE]

1 page this fax

TO: [   ]
FROM: [   ]
RE:

Dear [   ]:

After I meet with key clients and colleagues, I always summarize my notes and pass them by people to make sure I've accurately recorded what was discussed and what agreements were made.

During our phone conversation this morning, we discussed:

[point]

[point]

[point]

If you remember other things we covered, please call me by [deadline]. If I don't hear from you by then, I'll proceed following the action steps outlined here.

Thank you for your interest in [company].

Sincerely,

[Name]
[Title]

- **Use a confirming fax immediately after talking to a prospect you know who tends to forget things that have been agreed upon.**

- **Ask the prospect to get back to you if he or she disagrees with your outline of what is happening.**

Path on CD-ROM: Marketing/Sales→Sales→Faxing summary to someone who forgets→Faxing summary to someone who forgets—example 1

Faxing to a prospect about early deadline

[DATE]

1 page this fax

TO: [   ]
FROM: [   ]
RE:

Dear [   ]:

Space on our consulting calendar is filling fast for the next three months. If you are still interested in having us lead your [project] project, please phone soon so we can reserve you the necessary hours. Once all of our hours are filled up, we would have to defer working on your project until four months from now.

At the time we last talked, you said you were on the verge of moving forward with the [effort] effort. I just wanted to give you the opportunity to reserve *time with* us if you're ready to pursue the project at this time. The cost of not acting could be high, as your whole business is rapidly changing to the technology we know so well.

We expect to have filled our schedule by [deadline]. Please let us know before then if you would like to proceed.

Sincerely,

[Name]
[Title]

- Use a fax to help move a slow-deciding customer.

- Show the prospect what will be lost by waiting.

Path on CD-ROM: Marketing/Sales→Sales→Faxing to prospect about early deadline→Faxing to prospect about early deadline—example 1

Faxing to a prospect overseas

[DATE]

1 page this fax

TO: [   ]
FROM: [   ]
RE:

Dear [   ]:

We are extremely enthusiastic about [placing our products in your stores] in the [United Kingdom]. It seems like this partnership could [move a lot of inventory] for both of us.

Time zones make talking by phone difficult, so I am faxing you this request for the information we need to go forward. At your earliest convenience, would you fax me:

[document]

[document]

[document]

We've been looking [for an outlet for this product] in the [UK] for almost a year and are so pleased to have connected with you. We are confident that the [British markets] will be most enthusiastic about [buying these products].

Sincerely,

[Name]
[Title]

- **Use an overseas fax to show serious interest in doing business with a foreign company.**

- **Be specific about your request.**

Path on CD-ROM: Marketing/Sales→Sales→Faxing to prospect overseas→Faxing to prospect overseas—example 1

Finding the decision maker

[DATE]

[Name]
[Company]
[Address]
[City, State ZIP]

Dear [   ]:

This is an outstanding offer for:

[potential decision maker's title]s;

[potential decision maker's title]s; or

[potential decision maker's title]s.

If you are not one of these people, would you pass this letter along to someone who is? If you are, read on.

According to [credible source], [company] makes the [most economical and environmentally friendly product] on the market. May I show it to you?

I'll call next week to set up a time for your personal demonstration. Thank you for your consideration.

Sincerely,

[Name]
[Title]

- **Encourage that this letter get routed to likely decision makers.**

- **Pitch the product and a demonstration.**

Path on CD-ROM: Marketing/Sales→Sales→Finding decision maker→Finding decision maker—example 1

Following up after mailing a brochure

[DATE]

[Name]
[Company]
[Address]
[City, State ZIP]

Dear [   ]:

Several weeks ago you requested information on our line of [exclusive eyeglass frames] and we were pleased to send you our brochure.

Perhaps you have additional questions about the [high-end frames] we offer. To help you make the right decision, we are enclosing a sheet that answers the most commonly asked questions about our line.

We hope these questions and answers will be helpful. If you have additional questions, please feel free to contact me.

Sincerely,

[Name]
[Title]

- **Remind the prospect of the brochure.**

- **Provide additional information.**

Path on CD-ROM: Marketing/Sales→Sales→Following up after mailing brochure→Following up after mailing brochure— example 1

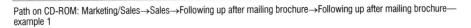

Following up on a sales proposal

[DATE]

[Name]
[Company]
[Address]
[City, State ZIP]

Dear [   ]:

Based on our recent conversations, I know that several of our payroll management solutions would greatly aid your company, especially as you continue to add employees.

You may recall that [three weeks] ago I sent you a proposal about the different ways [ABC Accounting Service] could help your company better manage its payroll. Although I haven't heard from you, I am writing to follow up how our company can act fast to help you address this critical need.

For instance, you expressed an urgency for [help tracking employees' time, as well as writing and distributing bi-weekly paychecks]. In the proposal, I said I could get the new arrangement set up and functioning within [two weeks] from your go-ahead. I can still guarantee that, from the time you say yes, it'll take [two weeks or less] for your solution to be in place.

I will call you later this week to answer any additional questions you have. Thank you for your interest in [ABC Accounting Service].

Sincerely,

[Name]
[Title]

- **Describe the proposal generally, explaining how it would solve (a) current customer problem(s).**

- **Show your concern by saying you will follow up.**

Path on CD-ROM: Marketing/Sales→Sales→Following up on sales proposal→Following up on sales proposal—example 1

Getting an appointment

[DATE]

[Name]
[Company]
[Address]
[City, State ZIP]

Dear [   ]:

Did you pay too much money into the federal government's tax coffers last year?

Many people—even those as savvy about their finances as you—did. The reason? The tax law offering new deductions was poorly understood. Shouldn't you take steps now, before the April 15 crunch, to get all the deductions you deserve for the current tax year?

Learn how to save money under the new law by using [Tax Planning Associates].

Let me show you how you can act now to save on taxes later. My service is low cost, especially when you consider how much money you'll save by using it! Over the past [15 years], I've worked with numerous families to help them better their tax situations under changing tax laws. I'd like to put my experience to work for you.

I'll call you next week to set up a convenient time to meet. To thank you for talking with me, this first meeting will be free. I look forward to helping you save money and meet your financial goals.

Sincerely yours,

[Name]
[Title]

- **Establish your credibility.**

- **Ask for the appointment.**

Path on CD-ROM: Marketing/Sales→Sales→Getting an appointment→Getting an appointment—example 1

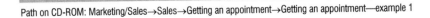

Getting a phone interview

[DATE]

[Name]
[Title]
[Company]
[Address]
[City, State ZIP]

Dear [   ]:

Do you wonder if your office staffers really make the most of their computer software? Do you think a training course on the packages you use could help improve their productivity?

If you said yes to either one of these questions, our custom training program is for you.

Would you give me just three minutes of your time on [Friday] to explain it to you? I'll call you then.

Sincerely,

[Name]
[Title]

- Ask for a specific amount of time.

- Make sure you follow up on the day you said you would.

Path on CD-ROM: Marketing/Sales→Sales→Getting phone interview→Getting phone interview—example 1

Introducing a new business

[DATE]

[Name]
[Company]
[Address]
[City, State, Zip]

Dear Neighbor:

I am pleased to announce the re-opening of [The Big Scoop Ice Cream], right around the corner from you at [57 Broad Street. We've doubled our size and now offer a big sit-in eating area, soft serve ice cream as well as the hard ice cream that we're famous for, and even a selection of fresh-baked pies.]

To celebrate our re-opening, we are having a celebration just for our close neighbors like you!

This [Friday] night from [6–8 p.m.] we'll have our opening offering [free dessert] for all! So bring your friends and come on down!

It's our way of saying thanks—for a great first season—and your patronage which has allowed us to expand [The Big Scoop.]

See you [Friday] night!

[The Big Scoop,]
[57 Broad Street]

- Offer special promotion to entice participation.

- End with a call to action.

Path on CD-ROM: Marketing/Sales→Sales→Introducing a new business→Introducing a new business—example 1

Introducing a new sales person

[DATE]

[Name]
[Company]
[Address]
[City, State ZIP]

Dear [   ]:

[He's not a bird or a plane, but a pilot.] This is but one of the many interesting things you can learn about our new [sales representative, Michael Golden], when he calls on you.

In addition to [flying twin-engine airplanes, Mike] has an excellent track record for providing clients the information they need. [He was previously a representative for Comp Repairs Unlimited and also volunteers his time with the United Way.]

We know you're going to enjoy meeting and working with [Mike]. If you have any questions, please don't hesitate to call.

Thank you for your continued business.

Sincerely,

[Name]
[Title]

- **Show the sales person's sales and service skills.**

- **Express confidence that this new relationship will work out just fine.**

Path on CD-ROM: Marketing/Sales→Sales→Introducing a new sales person→Introducing a new sales person—example 1

Introducing your replacement

[DATE]

[Name]
[Company]
[Address]
[City, State ZIP]

Dear [   ]:

I told my managers they had to hire someone really good as my replacement because that person would have to take really good care of you. Fortunately, they came through.

I'm really pleased with their choice of [name]. [S/he] has the same commitment to serving customers as I do. Plus, you'll benefit from tapping into [name]'s extensive knowledge of [area].

I'm going to miss meeting with you, [prospect]. I'd like to say good-bye and introduce you to [name] personally over lunch sometime in the next two weeks. I'll give you a call very soon to find out your schedule.

Sincerely,

[Name]
[Title]

- **Show that the new person has the same commitment to clients.**

- **Suggest a personal meeting.**

Path on CD-ROM: Marketing/Sales→Sales→Introducing replacement→Introducing replacement—example 1

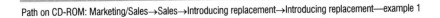

New product

[DATE]

[Name/Title]
[Business/Organization Name]
[Address]
[City, State ZIP]

Dear [   ]:

[JetPac] is here, and it may be just what you are looking for to help revolutionize your company's small engine construction and fuel distribution in the years to come.

Federal standards will make emission control compliance tougher for all forms of internal combustion engines. But in 1996, the Environmental Protection Agency will shift its sights from Detroit's automotive empire to small engine manufacturers throughout the country. Regulators plan to take the same tough standards they have set for automobiles and apply them to companies without the profit margins to support major retooling efforts. Of necessity, some of these companies will go out of business. Yours does not have to be one of those.

[JetPac] offers a patented fuel filtering and distribution system that removes [94] percent of all harmful and noxious gases from all sizes of internal combustion engines. Rather than requiring complete redesign and overhaul of the manufacturing process, [JetPac's] assembly procedures mesh with preexisting assembly line operations. The [JetPac] filter and manifold assembly fits easily over existing carburetors. An extra step, rather than a complete overhaul, is all that is required.

We have enclosed detailed literature describing the product's engineering specifications, and we urge you to study it closely. If you think your production line may have room for a [JetPac] assembler and you agree that your company will not survive without some form of greater emission controls, then call our toll-free number today and learn more about what [JetPac] can do to help position your product for the twenty-first century.

Sincerely,

[Name]
[Title]

- **Create a sense of urgency.**

- **End with a call to action.**

Path on CD-ROM: Marketing/Sales→Sales→New product→New product—example 1

Offering a membership

[DATE]

[Name]
[Company]
[Address]
[City, State ZIP]

Dear [   ]:

Looking for a way to meet people? To keep in shape? To learn a new sport?

A great way to do all three is by joining [club]. Our members can tell you, a [club] membership pays you back all year–and sometimes even longer.

"I'm sometimes afraid to admit it, but I met my husband at [club]."
–[member], [number]-year member

"The personal trainer helped me find a fitness program I could stick to."
–[member], [number]-year member

"I use the gym and the pool, but I also learned how to play racquetball and squash at [club]."
–[member], [number]-year member

With the cold weather approaching, it's a great time to take your exercise routine inside a club. Check out all the benefits of joining in the enclosed brochure. I'll give you a call next week to answer any questions and to set up your personal tour.

Sincerely,

[Name]
[Title]

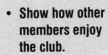

- **Show how other members enjoy the club.**

- **Tie the benefits of joining to a season or holiday, if appropriate.**

Path on CD-ROM: Marketing/Sales→Sales→Offering membership→Offering membership—example 2

Offering a referral

[DATE]

[Name]
[Title]
[Company]
[Address]
[City, State ZIP]

Dear [   ]:

[Allied Manufacturers] has been buying [rubber parts] from us for years. Recently, my contact there expressed a need for [legal services around patent issues] and I thought of you.

You can contact [Bernard Todd at Allied, 555/555-1839], and feel free to use my name. I hope this referral will prove fruitful for both of you.

Sincerely,

[Name]
[Title]

- **Choose carefully whom you refer to a longtime, important client.**

- **Provide a contact name and number.**

Path on CD-ROM: Marketing/Sales→Sales→Offering referral→Offering referral—example 2

Overcoming a prospect's past bad experience with your company

[DATE]

[Name]
[Company]
[Address]
[City, State ZIP]

Dear [   ]:

Every salesperson here at [company] tells me not to waste time writing to you because you've said time and time again that you don't want to do business with [company]. But no one can tell me why.

I asked our sales manager and he said he didn't know what had happened. I asked our current president, and he said he wished he knew. I even asked our company "historian" and he said to let him know if I found out.

Obviously it's been quite a long time since whatever happened. Many of the staff people here have changed. We are dedicated to quality product and excellent service. We have the best [product] line on the market and you'll make money and gain more customers if you offer it. Would you consider doing business with us again?

I'll call next week to see about setting up a meeting. I'm looking forward to meeting you.

Sincerely,

[Name]
[Title]

- If appropriate, show how old (and no longer worthwhile) the grudge is.

- Simply state how the prospect would do better business if he or she was doing business with you.

Path on CD-ROM: Marketing/Sales→Sales→Overcoming prospect's bad experience with company→Overcoming prospect's bad experience with company—example 1

Prospecting based on company being new in the area

[DATE]

[Name]
[Company]
[Address]
[City, State ZIP]

Dear [   ]:

We're new and, pleasantly, different.

Here at [company] we offer similar [products or services] than other [type of businesses] in the area. And yet, it's not just our newness to the area that makes us stand out.

• We offer experienced consultants to help you make your [type] decisions.
• We offer special savings to customers who do [amount] volume of business with us.
• We work with both individual and corporate clients.

Stop by or call our [office or store] now to learn about our special [name of promotion], going on from now until [deadline].

Sincerely,

[Name]
[Title]

• **Show the benefits to customers of your company being new and different.**

• **Offer a special incentive to get prospects to come to your store or office.**

Path on CD-ROM: Marketing/Sales→Sales→Prospecting based on company being new in area→Prospecting based on company being new in area—example 1

Prospecting a new member of the local chamber of commerce

[DATE]

[Name]
[Company]
[Address]
[City, State ZIP]

Dear [   ]:

Welcome to [city], and the [city] Chamber of Commerce, where members are known for helping each other out.

We know you're going to enjoy the fun and the business leads that come from being an active member of the Chamber. In fact, we want to get you started on the right foot. Just bring this letter with you when you come to our [location] for a free [consultation] consultation.

There's no obligation, just a chance to get to know a fellow member and to get our studied, yet honest opinion on [area].

If you have any questions, please feel free to call me. Look forward to meeting you in person!

Sincerely,

[Name]
[Title]

- **Welcome the person to the group.**

- **Offer an introductory consult or product or promotion to "get to know each other."**

Path on CD-ROM: Marketing/Sales→Sales→Prospecting new member of chamber of commerce→Prospecting new member of chamber of commerce—example 1

Prospecting religious leaders

[DATE]

[Name]
[Company]
[Address]
[City, State ZIP]

Dear [   ]:

As congregations get larger, helping new parishioners meet longtime members is key to maintaining a sense of community. Many area churches are finding that a church pictorial—a book of photos of church members—can really help people get to know one another better.

May we help you put together this useful community-building tool? There will be no cost to the church or to parishioners for the photo sittings. We'll photograph each individual that is interested, then compile the pictorial. The pictorials will be available for parishioners to purchase for $7 (10 percent of which we'll donate to the congregation.) Of course, parishioners can also purchase additional reprints of their portraits if they wish.

We're currently scheduling photo sittings during the month of [month]. I hope you'll call to reserve several times for your parishioners. Having a pictorial can be so useful to them as they strive to know their fellow members.

I'll call you next week to answer any questions you may have. In addition, I'll be able to provide the names of other ministers and priests who have used this service.

Sincerely,

[Name]
[Title]

- **Show how the service you offer will help the clergy person overcome current challenges.**

- **Show side benefits.**

Path on CD-ROM: Marketing/Sales→Sales→Prospecting religious leaders→Prospecting religious leaders—example 1

Prospecting someone recently appointed to a volunteer position

[DATE]

[Name]
[Company]
[Address]
[City, State ZIP]

Dear [   ]:

The [non-profit organization] couldn't be luckier in the appointment of you as its new board chairman. Your commitment to the community and the environment is unparalleled.

I know that one of the goals of [non-profit organization] this year is to renovate its offices in an environmentally and health-conscious fashion. I'd like to put my firm's [12] years of experience in green design and remodeling to work for you on this project.

I'll give you a call before the next board meeting to see how you're liking your new responsibilities and if we might be able to work together.

Sincerely,

[Name]
[Title]

- **Show your support for the person's volunteer work.**

- **Show your company's experience or past success with the kind of project you expect the charity will undertake.**

Path on CD-ROM: Marketing/Sales→Sales→Prospecting someone appointed to volunteer position→Prospecting someone appointed to volunteer position—example 1

Prospecting someone who just got a new job

[DATE]

[Name]
[Company]
[Address]
[City, State ZIP]

Dear [   ]:

Congratulations on your new job! We'd like to help you celebrate by scheduling a free sitting for your media portrait. Let's face it, people whose careers are growing need a great publicity photo on hand.

To further show our enthusiasm for your success, we'll give you a free 8 x 10 when you purchase pictures from the sitting.

Give us a call by [deadline] to set up a time for your free shoot. We look forward to seeing you.

Sincerely,

[Name]
[Title]

- **Offer the person something free and special in honor of the occasion.**

- **Show how both the job and your offer are steps up in the world.**

Path on CD-ROM: Marketing/Sales→Sales→Prospecting someone who just got new job→Prospecting someone who just got new job—example 1

Prospecting a technical professional

[DATE]

[Name]
[Company]
[Address]
[City, State ZIP]

Dear [   ]:

Only the most advanced software programmer at your company need attend.

But he or she definitely needs to attend.

At the upcoming [seminar event], to be held [time, date and place], already advanced programmers will gain even more insight into the following techniques:

[advanced technique 1]

[advanced technique 2]

[advanced technique 3]

[advanced technique 4]

You'll also get to network with advanced programmers from all over the country. Hurry! Because we must ensure lots of presenter-participant interactions, we only enroll 25 participants.

To register, simply complete the enclosed reply card with your credit card information. Or, if you prefer, you may register via the Web at [URL], or call us at [800 number].

If you're not the most senior programmer at your company, would you consider passing this letter along?

Sincerely,

[Name]
[Title]

- **Use more technical language to explain the product, service or course than you would in most sales letters.**

- **Write in a very linear fashion, matching the prospect's likely thinking pattern.**

Path on CD-ROM: Marketing/Sales→Sales→Prospecting technical professional→Prospecting technical professional—example 1

Prospecting a training manager

[DATE]

[Name]
[Company]
[Address]
[City, State ZIP]

Dear [   ]:

What's the main reason you haven't invested in time management training for your employees? Is it

a lack of time?

a lack of commitment from management?

a lack of ability to pull employees from their regular duties?

What if I told you that I provide a time management training that wouldn't cost you anything up front, make management put up a red flag, or take away from employees' work time? Would you call me?

Please do. I promise I'll only take five minutes of your time to explain how [company]'s training is ideal for you. Only if you're still interested after five minutes will we keep talking.

Sincerely,

[Name]
[Title]

- **Recognize and respond to the potential problems faced by training managers.**

- **Make a deal about how long you get to pitch before the trainer gets to say yes or no.**

Path on CD-ROM: Marketing/Sales→Sales→Prospecting training manager→Prospecting training manager—example 1

Prospecting with a contest

[DATE]

[Name]
[Company]
[Address]
[City, State ZIP]

Dear [   ]:

Here's your chance to show your skills at building design for people with disabilities—and to qualify for some special publicity.

[company] announces its [number] annual "Special Designs" contest. To enter, simply submit your plan for a community building that is totally handicapped accessible, and includes products from the [company] special remodeling line designed for creating accommodations for people with disabilities. The enclosed materials should answer your questions about how to enter.

Our panel of judges will select the final winner, who will be announced [date] at the [name of event or trade show] in [location]. The winner will be interviewed by industry magazine reporter, [name], who covers this contest each year. In addition, a cash prize of [dollars] will be awarded.

Don't miss the [deadline]! Send your designs in to this worthwhile contest today! If you have a question, please feel free to call me.

Sincerely,

[Name]
[Title]

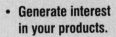

- **Generate interest in your products.**

- **Increase entries by offering good prizes and making it easy to enter.**

Path on CD-ROM: Marketing/Sales→Sales→Prospecting with contest→Prospecting with contest—example 2

Providing prospect information to a dealership

[DATE]

[Name]
[Company]
[Address]
[City, State ZIP]

Dear [   ]:

[prospect name] recently wrote us asking for information on where to [buy brand name products]. Because [he or she] lives in [area], we provided [him or her] with your [dealership] name and telephone number.

We have encouraged [name] to stop by your [showroom], however, we realize some people do not respond to this encouragement. Would you follow up by phoning [him or her]? It should be a win-win for all of us.

Thank you.

Sincerely,

[Name]
[Title]

- **Explain the referral that has occurred.**

- **Ask the dealership to follow up with the prospect.**

Path on CD-ROM: Marketing/Sales→Sales→Providing prospect information to dealership→Providing prospect information to dealership—example 1

Reminding that a sale is about to end

[DATE]

[Name]
[Company]
[Address]
[City, State ZIP]

Dear [   ]:

While our [Start of Summer] sale ends on [June 5], it's not yet too late to take advantage of some of the best prices of the season.

[In fact, in this last week of the sale, we're reducing prices an additional 25 percent!] Come in and take a look at the great [electronic] products we offer. You'll find just the right things for home or office.

Our [Start of Summer] sales flyer is enclosed. Please take a moment to look over the offerings and then come in to see us. You will be glad to get such good prices on [electronics] you need.

Sincerely,

[Name]
[Title]

- **Provide two reminders of the end of the sale, one at the start of the letter, the other at the close.**

- **Provide details of the sale, either in the letter or a separate sales flyer.**

Path on CD-ROM: Marketing/Sales→Sales→Reminding sale is about to end→Reminding sale is about to end—example 1

Requesting appointment after initial discussion

[DATE]

[Name]
[Company]
[Address]
[City, State ZIP]

Dear [   ]:

It was a pleasure meeting you at the [organization] meeting last week. I enjoyed talking ["golf"] and was also pleased that you shared your needs for [product or service].

As you can tell from our discussion at the meeting, I am the kind of sales person who doesn't sell just for the sake of selling. Rather, I'm interested in helping prospects and clients find real solutions to the challenges they face.

I think [company] could help you a lot. But I want to make sure. And, I want to determine in just what ways. That's why I think you and I should sit down soon to talk a bit more in length about your needs and what [company] can do to meet them.

I'll call you in a couple of days to see what time and date might be most convenient for you.

Sincerely,

[Name]
[Title]

- Remind the prospect of your initial discussion, using a personal touch if possible.

- Suggest a meeting to further flesh out the prospect's needs and how your company might be able to help.

Path on CD-ROM: Marketing/Sales→Sales→Requesting appointment after initial discussion→Requesting appointment after initial discussion—example 1

Requesting a meeting based on travel schedule

[DATE]

[Name]
[Company]
[Address]
[City, State ZIP]

Dear [   ]:

The prospect of [working with suppliers headquartered half way across the country] may seem like a hassle. But it's really not. Especially when they come to you.

I'm frequently in [prospect's city], as I will be on [dates]. Would you give me 15 minutes of your time to [show you our product line], and to explain how easy it would be to do business with [company]?

I'm enclosing some literature on the [aspects] aspects of the [company] [product]. Please look them over, and I'll call you in a couple of days to see if you have any questions and if you'd be interested in meeting while I'm in town.

Thanks for your consideration.

Sincerely,

[Name]
[Title]

- **Show how your visit is one of the benefits the prospect would get from doing business with your company.**

- **Suggest times to meet when you'll be in the prospect's city anyway.**

Path on CD-ROM: Marketing/Sales→Sales→Requesting meeting based on travel schedule→Requesting meeting based on travel schedule—example 2

Requesting a meeting with the true decision maker

[DATE]

[Name]
[Company]
[Address]
[City, State ZIP]

Dear [   ]:

Thank you for your interest in [company] and our products. As you might know, we are specialists in [specialization] and we can really help your company [achievement].

It would be marvelous to sit down and talk with you as you suggested, [time and date] in your office. I have made careful notes of your areas of interest: [area], [area] and [area], and will bring the information to our meeting.

You mentioned that you were collecting that data to help [name of decision maker] make the final decision. May I recommend that you invite [him or her] to this meeting? I'll be providing a lot of information that [s/he] is likely to appreciate hearing first hand.

If you have any questions before the meeting, please feel free to call me. Otherwise, I'll look forward to seeing you and [decision maker] on the [date]. Thanks again for your interest in [company].

Sincerely,

[Name]
[Title]

- **Explain that you will provide the information being sought.**

- **Suggest that the decision maker would be happy to be included in this meeting.**

Path on CD-ROM: Marketing/Sales→Sales→Requesting meeting with true decision maker→Requesting meeting with true decision maker—example 1

Rescheduling a sales appointment

[DATE]

[Name]
[Company]
[Address]
[City, State ZIP]

Dear [   ]:

I've just gotten word that our [lead research engineer] has been called away on [emergency family business].

Because of this situation, it is unlikely that I would have [a complete set of data] to share at our [date] meeting. As much as I enjoy meeting with you, I would like to suggest we postpone the meeting until all the data is ready.

As soon as I know [when the numbers will be crunched], I will give you a call to set up another meeting. Thank you for your understanding.

Sincerely,

[Name]
[Title]

- **Make it seem like an advantage to the prospect that you are rescheduling.**

- **Explain how a new meeting will be arranged.**

Path on CD-ROM: Marketing/Sales→Sales→Rescheduling sales appointment→Rescheduling sales appointment—example 1

Retaining customers

[DATE]

[Name]
[Title]
[Company]
[Address]
[City, State ZIP]

Dear [   ]:

We know you've been enjoying regular delivery of fresh produce from [Hann's Farm Markets]. Our records show your last scheduled delivery is [June 15].

Think about all the benefits of scheduling more deliveries:

- You don't have to go to the grocery store to choose from damaged, under- or over-ripe fruits and vegetables.
- You get our organically grown guarantee.
- You get great-tasting fruits and vegetables delivered right to your front door!

Consider the disadvantages:

Well, we can't honestly think of any. Unless you can, call us today to set up continued produce delivery from [Hann's]. You'll be in for some savory thymes!

Sincerely,

[Name]
[Title]

- **Point out the benefits of continuing to buy your product or service.**

- **Add a sense of urgency with an expiration date if possible.**

Path on CD-ROM: Marketing/Sales→Sales→Retaining customers→Retaining customers—example 1

Selling additional products

[DATE]

[Name]
[Company]
[Address]
[City, State ZIP]

Dear [   ]:

I was so glad to hear you're really pleased with the [current products] you are now buying from [company]. It is our pleasure to serve you.

In fact, if you're pleased with the [current product], you might also like to consider [new product]. It is manufactured to the same high quality standards as [current product].

I'm enclosing some literature on [new product]. Please take a moment to look it over and see if it would meet your needs. I'll give you a call next week to see if you have any questions.

Sincerely,

[Name]
[Title]

- **Open referring to past positive events in the sales relationship.**

- **Suggest that the customer might like to also consider the new product.**

Path on CD-ROM: Marketing/Sales→Sales→Selling additional products→Selling additional products—example 1

Selling additional services

[DATE]

[Name]
[Company]
[Address]
[City, State ZIP]

Dear [   ]:

It was really a pleasure researching your new market. I am excited that you have been able to run with several of the ideas included in my proposal. We make a great team!

Because of this I want to follow up with you about another project we had discussed: [project]. As with our first project, I am confident I could provide you with more ideas you can use—and the supporting research as well!

I'll give you a call next week to see if you are interested in proceeding.

Sincerely,

[Name]
[Title]

- **Use this kind of follow-up letter to encourage future business with the same client.**

- **Note the success of your previous work together.**

Path on CD-ROM: Marketing/Sales→Sales→Selling additional services→Selling additional services—example 1

Selling a business product

[DATE]

[Name]
[Company]
[Address]
[City, State ZIP]

Dear [   ]:

Tired of [the paper jamming in your copier]?

Guess you don't have the [copier product]. [Its special tray feeder design jams [percentage] less than other leading copiers.]

That translates to [less time spent fighting with the copier and more time spent making sales, coaching employees and closing successful business deals].

May I [invite you to our showroom for a personal demonstration]? I'll call you next week to set up a time.

Sincerely,

[Name]
[Title]

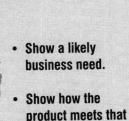

- Show a likely business need.

- Show how the product meets that need.

Path on CD-ROM: Marketing/Sales→Sales→Selling business product→Selling business product—example 1

Selling a consumer product

[DATE]

[Name]
[Company]
[Address]
[City, State ZIP]

Dear [   ]:

How many times lately have you wanted to use the phone, only to find that your teenage daughter is on an "important" three-hour call?

Imagine how great it would be to make a call whenever you want—and not have to compete with your children.

Now you can have it all at an affordable cost. [Telephone Ease Co.] can install a second phone line for your children. The line will give you the freedom to use the phone whenever you want to, no matter what calls your kids are making.

To find out more, simply call our toll-free number, [800/555-5555]. Our customer care representative will answer your questions and set up your second-line installation.

As a special bonus for calling now, you'll receive a long-distance phone card worth [$10] absolutely free, with no obligation to buy anything. Whatever you decide, the card is our gift to you just for calling.

Don't wait in line to use the phone! Call today. Remember, you get a free [$10] long-distance phone card just for responding to this offer.

Sincerely yours,

[Name]
[Title]

- **Show how your product or service can solve the potential customer's problem.**

- **Make a special offer before closing the letter.**

Path on CD-ROM: Marketing/Sales→Sales→Selling consumer product→Selling consumer product—example 1

Selling an educational seminar

[DATE]

[Name]
[Company]
[Address]
[City, State ZIP]

Dear [   ]:

Organizations around the world are feeling the pinch of the year 2000 computer glitch. It's an immovable deadline. While their boards of directors are unlikely to be computer experts, they may have real liability if organizations' systems fail at the turn of the new millennium.

That's why you should send your whole board of directors to the [company] workshop:

[title].

Led by compliance expert [name], you'll learn not only problem basics and accepted fix strategies, but also what you can do to protect yourself against potential lawsuits.

Plus, enjoy [destination city] when you join us [dates].

Please review the enclosed brochure detailing the seminar agenda and the background of the presenter. Then call us at [888 number] to register. Or, you can sign up via our Web site at [URL].

Sincerely,

[Name]
[Title]

P.S. Learn what your risk is! Register today!

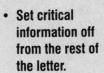

- **Set critical information off from the rest of the letter.**

- **Use a postscript to ask for the registration.**

Path on CD-ROM: Marketing/Sales→Sales→Selling educational seminar→Selling educational seminar—example 1

Selling membership renewal

[DATE]

[Name]
[Company]
[Address]
[City, State ZIP]

Dear [   ]:

Can you believe it's been a year already? You've become such an important member of [club] in such a short time.

[Name], [name] and [name] are all hoping you're planning to [play squash with them in this year's tournament]. And the front desk staff is hoping to keep hearing your cheerful whistle.

Renewing is easy. Just fill out the enclosed reply card and return it to us. We'll bill you later.

Looking forward to continuing to see you.

Sincerely,

[Name]
[Title]

- **Create a sense of belonging to encourage the member to renew.**

- **Make the process of renewing as easy as possible.**

Path on CD-ROM: Marketing/Sales→Sales→Selling membership renewal→Selling membership renewal—example 1

Selling a subscription

[DATE]

[Name]
[Company]
[Address]
[City, State ZIP]

Dear [   ]:

Did you know that [fact]? Or that [fact]? And that [fact]?

Get all this information and more with a special introductory subscription to [publication]. For just [amount], you can get [number] information-packed issues. That's [percentage] off the regular price. If you are dissatisfied in any way, we'll gladly stop your subscription.

Don't get left out! Get the facts. Get [publication].

To take advantage of this special introductory offer, simply call us at [800 #] or return the enclosed reply card.

Sincerely,

[Name]
[Title]

- **Use a catchy introductory paragraph.**

- **Offer a special rate to induce new subscribers.**

Path on CD-ROM: Marketing/Sales→Sales→Selling subscription→Selling subscription—example 1

Selling to a CEO

[DATE]

[Name]
[Company]
[Address]
[City, State ZIP]

Dear [   ]:

CEOs like you are charged with the heavy responsibility of setting the vision for their organizations. Once it's set, you need all the help you can get in making sure that vision penetrates every corner of every department, reaches the hearts and minds of every employee.

CEOs across the country are raving about what [company] has helped them do. With our all-staff programs in "How to Support a Vision" and "Adding Value to Vision," employees working for companies from New York to Los Angeles and from Minneapolis to Miami are getting on board with their leaders' visions—even enhancing them.

As I know you're about to finish your company-wide goal setting, may I suggest that this is the perfect time to arrange for "Vision" training for your staff? It's easy to do. Just give us a call at [phone number] and our trained staff will be glad to help.

By the way, I practice what I preach. Each year, my staff attends both "How to Support" and "Adding Value." It's made us an even more solid team.

Sincerely,

[Name]
[Title]

- Get your CEO to sign the letter; CEOs tend to like to deal with other CEOs.

- Make sure the product or service you are selling is worthy of the CEO's attention.

Path on CD-ROM: Marketing/Sales→Sales→Selling to CEO→Selling to CEO—example 1

Sending materials and suggesting another purchase

[DATE]

[Name]
[Company]
[Address]
[City, State ZIP]

Dear [   ]:

The plan you requested for [incorporating low-wall cubicles into your call center is enclosed].

You may also wish to consider the possible benefits of purchasing [special track lighting that Call Center Supplies Inc. offers. While the low-wall cubicles make nice work areas for call center employees, this track lighting is specially designed to help them see their work better.]

Please let me know if I can answer any questions for you. I would be glad to come by in person next week to talk about the different options.

Thank you for your interest in [Call Center Supplies].

Sincerely,

[Name]
[Title]

- **Provide the requested information.**

- **Suggest that the potential customer also purchase something else that would be useful.**

Path on CD-ROM: Marketing/Sales→Sales→Sending materials suggesting purchase→Sending materials suggesting purchase— example 1

Setting up an appointment

[DATE]

[Name/Title]
[Business/Organization Name]
[Address]
[City, State ZIP]

Dear [   ]:

If you have a free hour, I can show you a way to reduce the sorting and route management costs of your delivery business by up to [65] percent. Interested?

Those of us in the delivery business know that a fast sort of parcels and correspondence can make or break delivery time promises. Yet our greatest challenge is finding a sorting method that is fast, error-free, and relatively inexpensive. [TimeSplits] is offering a new technology that can help you solve your sorting problems without an expensive reengineering of your operation.

[TimeSplits'] new ZIP Sort adapts to existing routing systems while making use of basic personal computer technology to log, track, and route packages, parcels, and letters to both hub and isolated destinations. What's more, it reduces rather than increases dependence on staff to hand-sort misfiled items.

If you can spare an hour during the week of [August 16], I can show you a way to improve service while reducing costs. I guarantee it will be one of the best hours you will spend all year.

I will call next week to set up an appointment where we can discuss your needs in more detail. The future of mail and package sorting has arrived, and I would like you to be among the first to take advantage of this new technology.

Sincerely,

[Name]
[Title]

- **Describe how your service can benefit the company.**

- **Explain how you're going to follow up.**

Path on CD-ROM: Marketing/Sales→Sales→Setting up appointment→Setting up appointment—example 1

Soliciting a distributor for a product

[DATE]

[Name]
[Company]
[Address]
[City, State ZIP]

Dear [   ]:

[Perfect Binding Press] titles are finding their way into more and more bookstores, including [three national ones. We've got shelf space at Bound Books, Jelly Bean Books, and The Booksellers.]

[Bound Books is stocking four titles, Jelly Bean six, and The Booksellers two. This is in addition to the titles stocked by regional and local bookstores.]

We hope that as our progress continues, you'll become our distributor. We would particularly like to work with you because of your expertise in helping small presses grow.

Perhaps you'd like to talk about these retail developments further. I'll call you next week about the possibility of setting up a meeting.

Thank you for your consideration.

Sincerely,

[Name]
[Title]

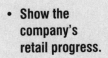

- Show the company's retail progress.

- Use flattery carefully.

Path on CD-ROM: Marketing/Sales→Sales→Soliciting distributor for product→Soliciting distributor for product—example 1

Soliciting a sale for a client's once-in-a-lifetime event

[DATE]

[Name]
[Title]
[Company]
[Address]
[City, State ZIP]

Dear [   ]:

Congratulations, graduate! You should be very proud of completing high school with the Class of [1998].

Photographs can help you remember this special time in your life. [Auble's Photo Studio] can take just the shots you need.

With a complete indoor studio and a wide range of outdoor possibilities, [Auble's] can photograph you with your violin—or your horse. We can capture your formal side—and your casual self. [We'll even throw in a free 8 x 10 enlargement of your favorite shot when you bring this letter to your sitting.]

The schedule for graduation photos books fast! Don't miss this opportunity to have them done at [Auble's].

Sincerely,

[Name]
[Title]

- **Open with congratulations on the special event.**

- **Make sure to include what makes your offering different from others.**

Path on CD-ROM: Marketing/Sales→Sales→Soliciting sale for once-in-a-lifetime-event→Soliciting sale for once-in-a-lifetime-event—example 1

Special prospecting techniques

[DATE]

[Name]
[Company]
[Address]
[City, State ZIP]

Dear [   ]:

Do you have what it takes to be a wine-tasting connoisseur? Our free Taster Talent Test can help.

Many people are interested in being wine experts, but few have the drive or the taste buds. Few are willing to taste enough wines. Few are prepared for the commitment to world travel necessary to reach famous and beautiful vineyards.

But maybe the rewards sound good to you. Find out your status with our free Taster Talent Test. Simply complete the enclosed questionnaire and return it to us. Within [three weeks], we'll send back a full analysis of your answers that will help you decide whether wine tasting is your future!

All of this is absolutely free. So send in your questionnaire today.

Sincerely,

[Name]
[Title]

- **Catch attention with a self-quiz.**

- **After qualifying the prospect, send related sales inquiries.**

Path on CD-ROM: Marketing/Sales→Sales→Special prospecting techniques→Special prospecting techniques—example 1

Thanking for a recommendation

[DATE]

[Name]
[Title]
[Company]
[Address]
[City, State ZIP]

Dear [   ]:

Thank you for sending us such a positive recommendation. I'm grateful for your continued confidence in [Morby's Luggage]. We'll continue to strive to serve you in the best way possible.

Thanks so much for being a customer.

Sincerely,

[Name]
[Title]

- Say thank you for the recommendation and for being a customer.

- Show your commitment to maintaining a high product and service standard.

Path on CD-ROM: Marketing/Sales→Sales→Thanking for recommendation→Thanking for recommendation—example 1

Tickler

[DATE]

[Name]
[Title]
[Company]
[Address]
[City, State ZIP]

Dear [   ]:

You came to mind this morning when I heard the news about the [flood]. How are you handling it?

Sincerely,

[Name]
[Title]

- **Keep a tickler short; your goal is to stay in the front of their minds, not to sell anything in this note.**

- **Relate what you know about the customer to the news to make a tickler personal.**

Path on CD-ROM: Marketing/Sales→Sales→Tickler→Tickler—example 1

Updating clients on new product features

[DATE]

[Name]
[Company]
[Address]
[City, State ZIP]

Dear [   ]:

Even as the year 2000 fix heats up under pressure, [Y2K Track] has released a new version chock full of features to better serve you.

Besides the already terrific guidelines for systems and processes to check, the new version also includes:

[•   Extra cells for documenting who did a particular test]
[•   An accompanying binder to guide your storage of an offsite hard copy of your work]
[•   Regular cues for making electronic backups of your work and moving them offsite]
[•   Better on-line help]
[•   Case studies from organizations that have been successful so far]

[Our contacts at several financial institutions are already using the new version—and they love it!]

To demonstrate to you just how excellent the software is, we'd like to send you a free demo kit. Give us a call at [800/555-3847] today!

Sincerely,

[Name]
[Title]

- **Add a sense of urgency to the need for this product.**

- **Detail the main features of the new product.**

Path on CD-ROM: Marketing/Sales→Sales→Updating clients on new product features→Updating clients on new product features—example 1

Updating sales people on mid-period sales performance (bad news)

INTEROFFICE MEMORANDUM

TO: [   ]
FROM: [Sales manager]
DATE: [   ]
SUBJECT: [Let's get creative]

Keep on keeping on, people! I know that I'm working with one of the best sales teams in the region. That's why we set our goals so high. Even though it looks like we're a long way from making our quarterly goal of [$5 million in pension sales], I know that when push comes to shove, you'll all reach into your bag of tricks and come up with just the sales we need. Go team!

- **Show you believe in the sales people's ability.**

- **End with encouragement.**

Path on CD-ROM: Marketing/Sales→Sales→Updating sales people on performance—bad news→Updating sales people on performance—bad news—example 1

Updating sales people on mid-period sales performance (good news)

INTEROFFICE MEMORANDUM

TO: [   ]
FROM: [Sales manager]
DATE: [   ]
SUBJECT: [You're on target for success!]

Way to go team! We're on track to meet our goal of [$5 million in new pension funds] for the quarter, having reached [$3.7 million with two weeks to go].

I know each of you will be working extra hard to wrap up loose ends and show off your closing skills during the last [14 days]. Go team!

- **Open and close with encouragement.**

- **Show your belief the goal can be made.**

Path on CD-ROM: Marketing/Sales→Sales→Updating sales people on performance good news→Updating sales people on performance—example 1

Using special prospecting techniques, example #1

[DATE]

[Name]
[Title]
[Company]
[Address]
[City, State ZIP]

Dear [   ]:

What do you want most in a [pair of sandals]?

[_Real leather straps?]

[_Buckles that last?]

[_Stylish design?]

When you buy at [Sandal City], you can choose a [pair of sandals] that meet these criteria—and many others.

In fact, [Sandal City] has the largest selection of [sandals] in town. [Mention this letter and get a 15 percent discount when you buy two pairs!]

Sincerely,

[Name]
[Title]

- **Use a checklist to help readers think about their needs and to help them move quickly into the letter.**

- **Consider offering special savings to those who read all the way to the bottom.**

Path on CD-ROM: Marketing/Sales→Sales→Using special prospecting techniques→Using special prospecting techniques—example 1

Using special prospecting techniques, example #2

[DATE]

[Name]
[Title]
[Company]
[Address]
[City, State ZIP]

Dear [   ]:

Several days ago you received a preliminary letter regarding the upcoming [textile industry group] meeting in [June]. Enclosed you will find a brochure with the details of the goals and sessions of the gathering, which will be held at the [Hotel Mont Marc].

We hope that you will be able to send a representative from your company to the event. Please feel free to call me if you have any questions.

Thanks for considering supporting your peers in the [textile] industry.

Sincerely,

[Name]
[Title]

- **In the second letter, provide details, perhaps in an accompanying brochure.**

- **Ask for a commitment.**

Path on CD-ROM: Marketing/Sales→Sales→Using special prospecting techniques→Using special prospecting techniques— example 11

Welcome a new subscriber

[DATE]

[Name]
[Company]
[Address]
[City, State ZIP]

Dear [   ]:

In a matter of days you should be receiving your first copy of [publication]. With its arrival you will join an exclusive group of the most informed people in the [region].

We are pleased to welcome you as a new subscriber and are confident that you will be very pleased with the [type of publication]. If you have any questions or concerns, please feel free to contact us.

Sincerely,

[Name]
[Title]

- **Build the excitement about becoming a new subscriber.**

- **Offer to answer any questions.**

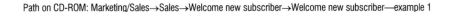

Path on CD-ROM: Marketing/Sales→Sales→Welcome new subscriber→Welcome new subscriber—example 1

Welcoming a new customer

[DATE]

[Name]
[Title]
[Company]
[Address]
[City, State ZIP]

Dear [   ]:

Welcome to [WELCO Rubber Products]. We're pleased you've decided on [WELCO] as your [replacement part] provider.

Within the week, you should be receiving a complete orientation kit from our customer service department. If you do not receive one, please let us know. If you have any questions now or when you receive the kit, please feel free to call us.

We know you'll be happy with [WELCO] because of our commitment to quality and on-time delivery.

Once again, welcome! Thanks for choosing [WELCO].

Sincerely,

[Name]
[Title]

- **Provide new customer orientation information, or explain how it will be provided.**

- **Remind the customer of why their choice is a good one.**

Path on CD-ROM: Marketing/Sales→Sales→Welcoming new customer→Welcoming new customer—example 1

Marketing

Technology has increased the number of avenues for reaching prospective customers, yet the traditional means—advertising, direct marketing, and surveys—are just as important as ever. More significant, technology has improved companies' abilities to target messages to the people most interested in their products and services. Sophisticated databases and order tracking have enabled businesses to better personalize their sale and marketing efforts and to more often engage in one-to-one marketing. Technology also has made selling additional products and services (cross-marketing) to customers much easier.

Meanwhile, the basic guidelines for communicating successfully with prospects have changed little over the years:

- Establish a connection with the prospect. Maybe she visited your company's booth at a trade show or has purchased other products similar to those your company manufactures.
- Use you-centered language and emphasize the benefits your product or service will bring the prospect.
- Entertain the prospect. Use action verbs. Do not send dull, wordy, or unclear messages.
- Be timely in your communications and give your prospect reasons to respond quickly.
- Ask for what you want: an order or a request for more information about your product or services.

Advertising

How regularly does your company advertise? How much advertising does it purchase? Your answers will help determine whether you handle your company's advertising needs in-house or contract with an independent copywriter or agency.

In dealing with the media, independent copywriters, and advertising/public relations firms, keep the following tips in mind:

- Before requesting information or proposals, complete a general media plan. Be flexible about the specifics, but decide whether you want full service from an agency or assistance only with one or a few specific projects.
- Allocate your advertising budget in advance.
- Clearly communicate your needs and expectations to the freelance writer or agency.
- When selecting a writer or agency, look for one who can relate to and work within your company's culture, as well as one who can sell your products or services.
- After you have selected a writer or agency, communicate regularly and carefully monitor progress. Point out any problems that may develop.

Agency hiring

[DATE]

[Name]
[Company]
[Address]
[City, State ZIP]

Dear [   ]:

We are pleased to inform you that we have selected your agency to handle our image-building campaign beginning [May 1 and ending October 31].

While we liked the innovative ideas in your detailed and comprehensive proposal, we do have several points we would like to discuss with your staff in person. Please call to schedule a meeting, so that we can provide your staff with additional background on [our bank] and finalize our agreement.

Thank you for your highly creative promotional ideas. We look forward to seeing them realized this year.

Sincerely,

[Name]
[Title]

- **Letter immediately announces the positive response.**

- **Close anticipates a productive agency agreement.**

Path on CD-ROM: Marketing/Sales→Advertising→Agency hiring→Agency hiring—example 1

Agency rejected

[DATE]

[Name]
[Company]
[Address]
[City, State ZIP]

Dear [   ]:

Thank you for presenting your advertising plan for [company] to our commu-nications team. While your presentation was a strong runner-up, we have decided to hire another firm that has more experience in the [medical prod-ucts] industry.

We will retain your materials on file and keep you in mind when future projects arise.

Sincerely,

[Name]
[Title]

- **Select another firm, instead of rejecting the reader's company.**

- **Explain crucial factors in the decision.**

Path on CD-ROM: Marketing/Sales→Advertising→Agency rejected→Agency rejected—example 1

Agency review

[DATE]

[Name]
[Company]
[Address]
[City, State ZIP]

Dear [   ]:

Now that we have been working with your advertising agency for almost a year, I would like to review our progress. Market response to our promotions has been less than forecast, and I would like to analyze these results in order to make necessary adjustments to future [company] promotions. This analysis will also be helpful in determining whether to continue our relationship with your agency.

I suggest we meet at [10:00 a.m.] on [date] to review our past promotional efforts. Please confirm if this time is convenient.

Sincerely,

[Name]
[Title]

- **State your intention and the reason for the review.**

- **Request confirmation of the receipt of this message and the suggested meeting time.**

Path on CD-ROM: Marketing/Sales→Advertising→Agency review→Agency review—example 1

Agency termination

[DATE]

[Name]
[Non-Profit Association]
[Address]
[City, State ZIP]

Dear [   ]:

When our charitable organization signed the contract with your marketing agency, we envisioned a smooth working relationship between your agency and our office. Unfortunately, the arrangement has not worked out. [Besides frequent miscommunications between agency professionals and our PR staff, agency expenses have run 25 percent or more above the estimates for each of the past four months.]

This letter provides the 30-day written notice of the termination of our agreement, as specified in the contract. Our organization will pay for agency services through the end of the month and will expect to receive the [completed, stage-two press packet by that date, as well as all photos, artwork, and ancillary materials developed in support of our ongoing $5-million capital campaign].

We regret that our agreement did not work out as we all had hoped it would.

Sincerely,

[Name]
[Title]

- Writer lists expectations firmly but not in a challenging manner.

- Letter states the unhappy facts without blaming any particular individual.

ADVERTISING

Competition

[DATE]

[Name/Title]
[Business/Organization Name]
[Address]
[City, State ZIP]

Dear [   ]:

It looks to us like you may have really put your foot in it this time, and we are not above asking for legal assistance in getting a cease-and-desist order. But let's try it the friendly way first.

Your recent shopper ad offers direct comparisons to our firm, claiming rates we do not offer, service problems not characteristic of us, and customer complaints we were not privy to. In the spoken word, that type of false and damaging information is called slander. When it appears in print, it is libel. And we want it stopped.

If the ad in question ever appears anywhere again, our attorney is prepared to file a libel suit immediately. If it does not reappear, we are willing to drop the whole thing. But we also would advise you not to make this a habit. Some competitors are even more vehement about such things than we are and may not give you fair warning.

Regards,

[Name]
[Title]

- **Identify the problem specifically.**

- **Make it clear the actions you will take if the behavior does not stop.**

Path on CD-ROM: Marketing/Sales→Advertising→Competition→Competition—example 1

Confidentiality agreement

[DATE]

[Name]
[Company]
[Address]
[City, State ZIP]

Dear [   ]:

This confirms our nondisclosure agreement:

[1. We agree that "confidential information" refers to any information provided to you by [company].]

[2. You agree not to use, share, or disseminate any confidential information with employers, clients, or anyone else.]

[3. You agree to use reasonable care in safeguarding the security of our confidential information.]

[4. You will not publish, copy, or disclose confidential information to any third party and will use reasonable caution in inadvertently disclosing any information to a third party.]

[company]   [name]

Signature _____   Signature _____

Date _____   Date _____

- **Consider the alternative of including a nondisclosure requirement as part of the primary contract with a freelance writer or agency.**

- **Also consider whether you want to add a noncompete clause or agreement, prohibiting the writer or agency from working simultaneously for one of your competitors.**

Path on CD-ROM: Marketing/Sales→Advertising→Confidentiality agreement→Confidentiality agreement—example 1

ADVERTISING

Request for bus rates

[DATE]

[Name]
[Company]
[Address]
[City, State ZIP]

Dear [   ]:

We are interested in advertising our [series of outdoor concerts] on [city] buses in [month/year].

Please write or call me at [223-4567] to provide rates and print specifications. What are the dimensions of the posters appearing on the buses? What paper stock is required?

Thank you.

Sincerely,

[Name]
[Title]

- **Consider public transportation, posters, table tents, place mats, scoreboards and all other alternative forms of communicating when planning advertising and public relations strategies.**

- **Ask for the required dimensions of the posters.**

Path on CD-ROM: Marketing/Sales→Advertising→Request for bus rates→Request for bus rates—example 1

ADVERTISING

Request for electronic rates

[DATE]

[Name]
[Company]
[Address]
[City, State ZIP]

Dear [   ]:

Our firm, [which produces time management and call tracking software], recently completed its marketing plan for the year ahead. We intend to purchase advertising on several business Web sites and are considering the addition of your magazine's Web site to our advertising mix.

Please send your Web site advertising rate card, including rates for a one-time monthly listing and multiple month listing options. In addition, we would like to know the number of hits your Web site has received for each of the past six months and whether there is a price discount if we also advertise in your print magazine. If there is a discount for advertising in both media, please also send an advertising rate card for the print publication.

Many thanks for your prompt response. We will begin our new advertising campaign two months hence.

Sincerely,

[Name]
[Title]

- **Writer saves time later by listing all the questions he needs answered now.**

- **Letter is specific and brief.**

Path on CD-ROM: Marketing/Sales→Advertising→Request for electronic rates→Request for electronic rates—example 1

ADVERTISING

Request for outdoor rates

[DATE]

[Name]
[Company]
[Address]
[City, State ZIP]

Dear [   ]:

[Company] is interested in learning about your rates and the availability of bill-boards on [highway], [highway], and [highway] leading into [city]. We hope to place outdoor advertising at these locations during [November and December].

Please call me at [444-3434] to discuss what is available at what rates.

Thank you.

Sincerely,

[Name]
[Title]

- **Mention the dates and locations you are interested in.**

- **Plan ahead to ensure that at least some of the locations you want will be available and to allow time to produce the advertising.**

Path on CD-ROM: Marketing/Sales→Advertising→Request for outdoor rates→Request for outdoor rates—example 1

Request for presentation

[DATE]

[Name]
[Company]
[Address]
[City, State ZIP]

Dear [   ]:

Thank you for your effort in submitting a proposal for our image-building promotional campaign. Your proposal certainly is one of the best that we received.

In order to make the best decision possible, we are inviting your agency to present your proposal to a committee of our officers and directors next week. We also are extending this invitation to [two] other agencies.

If you are interested in taking this additional step in our agency selection process, please call [Katherine Morphy at 222-222-2222] to arrange a time for your presentation.

We much appreciate the extra effort involved in this additional step. We also look forward to meeting your team and learning more about your promotional ideas for our [bank].

Sincerely,

[Name]
[Title]

- **Introduction lets the agency know that it produced an excellent proposal.**

- **Close assumes the agency will take the additional step of preparing a verbal presentation.**

Path on CD-ROM: Marketing/Sales→Advertising→Request for presentation→Request for presentation—example 1

ADVERTISING

Request for print rates

[DATE]

[Name]
[Company]
[Address]
[City, State ZIP]

Dear [   ]:

Our firm, which [produces time management and call tracking software], recently completed its marketing plan for the year ahead. We intend to purchase advertising in several small business publications and are considering the addition of your magazine to our advertising mix.

Please send your advertising rate card, including rates for one-time insertion, multiple insertion plans, and spot color options. We would also like to receive current circulation figures on your magazine and, if available, subscriber analysis by type and size of business.

Many thanks for your prompt response. We will begin our new advertising campaign [two months hence].

Sincerely,

[Name]
[Title]

- A brief explanation of the purpose of the proposed advertising demonstrates the legitimacy of the request.

- Close stresses the importance of a speedy response.

Path on CD-ROM: Marketing/Sales→Advertising→Request for print rates→Request for print rates—example 1

Request for proposal

[DATE]

[Name]
[Company]
[Address]
[City, State ZIP]

Dear [   ]:

Enclosed is a copy of our company newsletter, [*Employee Emissary*]. As I mentioned on the phone yesterday, we are considering the possibility of outsourcing the production of this newsletter.

It is published monthly. We would like each [four-page issue to contain a message from the president, one employee profile, and a list of upcoming company events, as well as tips on such generic organizational topics as time management, staying healthy, and team building strategies].

We would like a quote from you for writing, editing, and laying out the publication using [PageMaker] or other design software, so that each issue could go directly from your office to the printer without any intermediate steps.

Let me know if you are interested and what your price would be for these services. Call me if you have any questions.

Sincerely,

[Name]
[Title]

- **Enclosing a sample product answers many questions about the nature of the work requested.**

- **The writer delineates the general outline of the newsletter's content but gives the agency control over the details.**

Path on CD-ROM: Marketing/Sales→Advertising→Request for proposal→Request for proposal—example 1

Bidding Process

Most business owners and managers no longer sell their products or services based on a verbal agreement sealed with a handshake. Yet many products and services can still be sold through a simple letter of agreement. More extended agreements or arrangements with government agencies or corporations necessitate a formal contract. In either case, more is often at stake than just the current project. Successfully bidding and negotiating sales agreements can lead to a new, long-term client relationship or develop business contacts in new market niches.

You can effectively bid on and negotiate more and better contracts by doing the following:

- Increase your inquiries to potential clients. Provide a brief overview of your services and entice the reader with an offer to send additional information.
- Refer to the RFP or specific project in your introductory and cover letters.
- In developing the agreement, specify precisely what each party will do.
- Specify all terms, including the timing of payments.
- When there is a difference about specifications or terms, suggest alternative solutions.
- Ask any germane questions not covered in the information provided by the prospect.
- Demonstrate your interest in, and understanding of, the assignment.
- Close by describing a productive outcome and repeating your interest in doing business with the reader.

Acceptance of bid

[DATE]

[Name/Title]
[Business/Organization Name]
[Address]
[City, State ZIP]

Dear [   ]:

Our [executive staff] has reviewed your bid to [manage Xypro Industries' system needs using the Wacker 4000]. After careful examination of your [engineering] specifications and bid evaluation, we are pleased to report that we accept your offer.

We expect [the system to be functional] no later than [September 1]. Please coordinate the necessary timing and installation needs with [Operations Manager Carl Pelky. He will provide the coordinates and schematics you will need to complete the installation and test runs.]

Thank you for your interest in [Xypro]. We look forward to putting the [Wacker 4000 through its paces].

Sincerely,

[Name]
[Title]

- **Detail exactly what you expect and when.**

- **Identify your contact person.**

Path on CD-ROM: Marketing/Sales→Bidding-Negotiations→Bids→Bids—example 2

Asking questions in response to a request to bid

[DATE]

[Name]
[Company]
[Address]
[City, State ZIP]

Dear [   ]:

We appreciate the opportunity to bid on your [security project] and have three questions on the process as outlined in [RFP 19563]:

[1. Do you want a specific number of surveillance cameras installed around the perimeter of the property, or is this left to our recommendation?]

[2. What is the length of the perimeter?]

[3. How many employees required key cards?]

Your answers to these questions will help us provide the most accurate bid possible. I will call you on [Friday] to learn your answers.

Your corporation has a wonderful reputation in the community, and we are excited about the prospect of doing business with you.

Sincerely,

[Name]
[Title]

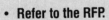

- **Refer to the RFP.**

- **Use the questions as an opportunity to repeat your interest in the project.**

Path on CD-ROM: Marketing/Sales→Bidding process—Negotiation→Asking questions in response to request to bid→Asking questions in response to request to bid—example 1

122

Confirming terms

[DATE]

[Name]
[Company]
[Address]
[City, State ZIP]

Dear [   ]:

Thank you for selecting our firm to print your magazine this year. We are excited about producing such a well-respected publication.

As you begin to draft our contract, we want to clarify our terms. [Company] offers [a 2 percent discount on your invoice if payment is received within 30 days of delivery. We hope this policy affords some assistance to your budget.]

We appreciate this opportunity to work with you and will review and return your contract as soon as possible.

Sincerely,

[Name]
[Title]

- **Explain your terms in a positive fashion. Some customers are more inclined to pay within 30 days to receive a discount than to avoid an interest charge that begins to accrue after that date.**

- **Promise to act on the contract as soon as you receive it.**

BIDDING PROCESS

Cover letter to a revised quote

[DATE]

[Name]
[Company]
[Address]
[City, State ZIP]

Dear [   ]:

I was pleased that you liked the detail and strength of our initial proposal for sales training for your customer service representatives.

Enclosed is a revised proposal, [eliminating the role play exercises, which you indicated your in-house training coordinator could facilitate in follow-up sessions]. As you can see, this change results in a [15 percent] price reduction.

I hope our sales training is now within your budget and that we will soon be helping your employees increase your company's bottom line.

Sincerely,

[Name]
[Title]

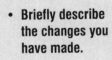

- Briefly describe the changes you have made.

- Explain how you will benefit the company's goals.

Path on CD-ROM: Marketing/Sales→Bidding process—Negotiation→Cover letter to revised quote→Cover letter to revised quote—example 2

Making bids and quotes

[DATE]

[Name]
[Company]
[Address]
[City, State ZIP]

Dear [   ]:

Thank you for asking: We are happy to submit this proposal to handle your accounting services. As a growing business in a competitive market, [Falcon Freight Lines] needs an accounting firm that offers personal service at a cost-effective price. This is exactly what we offer.

Unlike the large national firms, we will assign your account to senior, highly experienced partners. As a small firm, we have the flexibility and resourcefulness needed to respond to all deadlines, including those imposed by industry regulators. Like your own business, our firm has succeeded by doing what it takes to help its clients meet their goals.

The focus of our service will be [on compiling the year-end reports necessary for regulatory compliance and on minimizing tax liabilities for Falcon Freight and its owners.] Well-conducted tax and audit services combined with a strategic business plan can help you manage your business for continued growth.

The enclosed fee schedule quotes a fixed price for handling different types of tax returns as well as quarterly consultations billed on an hourly basis. As you can see, our prices are lower than what you might expect for the same services at a national firm.

We're looking forward to working with you and serving your accounting needs as your business expands in the years to come.

Sincerely,

[Name]
[Title]

- **Writer expresses ideas from the reader's point of view.**

- **Letter demonstrates an understanding of the client's tax and regulatory environment.**

Path on CD-ROM: Marketing/Sales→Bidding process—Negotiation→Making bids and quotes→Making bids and quotes—example 1

Proposal cover letter

[DATE]

[Name]
[Company]
[Address]
[City, State ZIP]

Dear [   ]:

We are submitting the enclosed proposal to [provide total quality management training to administrators of the Western Region Firefighters Association, in response to your recent RFP #8714. We can offer on-site instruction by an experienced team of TQM facilitators who have worked with scores of organizations over the past decade.]

As the proposal demonstrates, we have established an excellent record in [facilitating continuous improvement processes in diverse organizations, including more than a dozen security and firefighters associations. Post-training surveys of participants have shown that most rate our instructors at the A or A+ level and indicate they can easily apply what they have learned to their work situations.]

[We strengthen the on-site training experience with Power Point and video presentations, and manuals including all graphic materials are available for participants who miss a session or two. Participants report that the manuals are also a useful reference in later applying the TQM tools they have learned in our workshops.]

We are eager to meet your administrative staff members and begin putting our knowledge to work for the [Western Region Firefighters Association.]

Sincerely,

[Name]
[Title]

- **Cover letter refers to the RFP number.**

- **Letter summarizes key selling points of the proposal.**

Path on CD-ROM: Marketing/Sales→Bidding process—Negotiation→Proposal cover letter→Proposal cover letter—example 1

Proposal example

[DATE]

[Name]
[Company]
[Address]
[City, State ZIP]

Dear [   ]:

I am glad to offer this proposal for developing a direct mail package for your [software products for small business owners].

After reviewing the background materials you provided, [I suggest a traditional package, consisting of an outer, business-size envelope, four-page cover letter, brochure, order card, and business reply return envelope]. I will write this package and provide marketing and editorial support as needed to implement the project.

My estimate for these services is [$10,000]. This fee is based on working [100] hours at my hourly rate of [$100] and covers audience research, copy-writing, editing, teleconferencing, and consulting.

I will itemize direct expenses, for example, long distance telephone calls, fax charges, photocopies, and out-of-town travel related to the project, and pro-vide a separate invoice.

Reimbursement for expenses will be made within [10] days of receipt of invoice. Payment of the base fee will be made in three installments: one third at the beginning of the project, one third at the delivery of the first draft, and one third at the delivery of the final draft.

I appreciate the opportunity to submit this estimate. I hope to provide a pack-age for you that out-pulls your control for these products.

Sincerely,

[Name]
[Title]

- **Use a letter to convey short, uncomplicated proposals.**

- **Specify all terms, including the timing of payments.**

Path on CD-ROM: Marketing/Sales→Bidding process—Negotiation→Proposal→Proposal—example 1

Request for deadline extension

[DATE]

[Name]
[Company]
[Address]
[City, State ZIP]

Dear [   ]:

Yesterday I received your letter inviting [company] to quote on providing all of the [fixtures you need for your new store on the north side]. We are very interested in submitting a bid on your project.

Since we only received your notice yesterday, we are requesting an extension of the deadline by [two] days. We can have our bid to you by [date].

Please let me know if that date is acceptable. I have given your specifications and other background information to our estimator, to begin working on your bid.

I hope we can provide the [fixtures] you need at a price that meets your budget.

Sincerely,

[Name]
[Title]

- **Explain the reason for the request for a deadline extension.**

- **Plan to follow up by phone if you do not receive a response soon.**

Path on CD-ROM: Marketing/Sales→Bidding process—Negotiation→Request for deadline extension→Request for deadline extension—example 1

Requesting opportunity to quote

[DATE]

[Name]
[Company]
[Address]
[City, State ZIP]

Dear [   ]:

[Almost a year ago, I launched [company], a franchise of a national sign-making business. Using computer-aided design software, we now produce banners, posters, and billboards for scores of area organizations each week.]

I would like the opportunity to quote on providing the banners that your performing arts center regularly hangs on the front of the facility prior to performances.

Enclosed is a small-scale sample of our work, a recent table-top banner used at [organization's] annual meeting.

I will call you next week to learn the number and types of banners and other signs you will be needing this year.

I look forward to the opportunity to quote on the signs you need and to providing you with many high quality banners throughout the next performing arts season.

Sincerely,

[Name]
[Title]

- **Enclose a product sample, list of satisfied customers or other documentation of past successes.**

- **Demonstrate your interest by offering to take the next step — in this case, a telephone call.**

Path on CD-ROM: Marketing/Sales→Bidding process—Negotiation→Requesting opportunity to quote→Requesting opportunity to quote—example 1

Submitting contracts

[DATE]

[Name]
[Company]
[Address]
[City, State ZIP]

Dear [   ]:

I am pleased to return to you the signed contract for interior decorating ser-vices in the [lobby and meeting rooms of your headquarters office].

All clauses were clear and in accordance with our earlier discussions.

I appreciate the opportunity of refurbishing these spaces. I will begin prelimi-nary sketches immediately and will call you next week to set a time to show you the sketches and sample materials.

Sincerely,

[Name]
[Title]

- Letter specifies the topic of the contract.

- Close promises to begin work immediately and report on progress soon.

Path on CD-ROM: Marketing/Sales→Bidding process—Negotiation→Submitting contracts→Submitting contracts—example 1

Submission of bid

[DATE]

[Name/Title]
[Business/Organization Name]
[Address]
[City, State ZIP]

Dear [   ]:

Thank you for letting us review [Xypro Industries'] inventory management system needs. We are impressed with your current operation and feel we have just the system to meet your needs.

The [Wacker 4000] provides ample avenues for system management data, plus handling bays and digital storage capabilities designed to keep recordkeeping to a minimum. In addition to managing data through CD-ROM, the [Wacker 4000] provides the type of material handling that offers employees a safe working environment. Our automatic telephone system also processes incoming work orders and inquiries with minimal staff involvement.

The list price on the [Wacker 4000 is $34,695]. But we are pleased to offer it at a demonstration price of [$28,375]. That includes installation and up to six training sessions for up to ten primary staff members. Additional training is available and billable at [$75] per hour. On-line assistance is available at [$9] per half-hour.

We believe the [Wacker 4000] is the answer to your systems management needs. Please call us with your decision within ten days so we may put the technology of the future to work for you.

Best regards,

[Name]
[Title]

- **Explain exactly what products and services are being offered and for what price.**

- **End with a call to action.**

Path on CD-ROM: Marketing/Sales→Bidding—Negotiation→Bids→Bids—example 1

Direct Marketing

Reaching prospective customers directly is possible through the mail and telephone. The Telephone Consumer Protection Act of 1991, enforced by the Federal Communications Commission, prohibits sending unsolicited, electronic advertisements by fax or email without the permission of the recipient or an established business relationship. An individual who has signed on to a specific email list is presumably interested in receiving products and services related to the topic of that list.

Despite the appellation "junk mail," many business and individual customers respond to direct marketing, by returning a reply card, phone in, or faxing the order in sometimes as long as eight or more pages; a brochure or leaflet; an order card; and a return envelope. Of course, there is an infinite number of variations to the package and its design. For example, many packages contain a "lift letter," usually a small, folded note that often begins, "Read this only if you decide **not** to order." The prospect lifts the page to read additional sales copy, such as a special note from the editor of a publication. A "buck slip" is a dollar bill-shaped note with sales copy on the front and back.

The goal of all these pieces is to attract the attention of the reader, explain a product or service, and get a response in the form of a sale. Some direct marketing efforts initiate instead a two-step sale, requesting an inquiry from the reader that may lead to a sale. For instance, a reader might respond by asking for a free booklet or product sample (step one). If he likes the sample, the prospect will then buy the product (step two).

Unlike most business communications, which aim for efficiency, sales-oriented writing calls for a great deal of creativity and skill. It also is usually more informal. The use of contractions, sayings, stories, and breezy language can help pull the reader into the message.

To motivate readers to respond to your direct marketing, consider the following advice:

- Begin with a teaser, question, or other attention-grabber.
- Use colorful descriptions to appeal to the reader's sense of smell, sight, sound, and touch.
- Do not simply list the benefits of your service or product. Explain them as specific selling points in you-centered language. (You are not simply selling a reliable bicycle. You are selling a low-maintenance bicycle that the reader can use for commuting and weekend jaunts without worry.)
- Include a guarantee if you offer one.
- Provide all of the key information—what, when, where, and why.
- Consider using testimonials, stories, and personal references to add to your credibility.
- Consider offering a free booklet or other gift with the order.
- End with a strong action statement, such as, "order today" or "send for your free sample now."

Announcing a special sale

[DATE]

[Name]
[Company]
[Address]
[City, State ZIP]

Dear [   ]:

It's an exclusive once-a-year event. And you're invited. Don't miss [Steward's] preferred customer day on [Sept. 4].

Only [Steward's] top customers are invited to this event each year. The store closes from [8 p.m. to 10 p.m.] for everyone except special invitees like your-self, who will be warmly welcomed. You will get the opportunity to take advantage of special sales, meet the sales management team, and enjoy great refreshments and entertainment.

Please join us for this event. We appreciate your business!

Sincerely,

[Name]
[Title]

- **Make these customers feel special.**

- **Thank them for their business.**

Path on CD-ROM: Marketing/Sales→Direct marketing→Announcing a special sale→Announcing a special sale—example 1

DIRECT MARKETING

Announcing a new catalog

[DATE]

[Name]
[Company]
[Address]
[City, State ZIP]

Dear [   ]:

With Mother's Day just around the corner, we know you already have her gift and card purchased, wrapped, and ready. What, you don't?

Let the new [Great Gifts] catalog make your Mother's Day shopping a breeze. Flip through the pages of products chosen with mom in mind. Choose the perfect greeting card. And, get it gift wrapped and delivered to mom's door. All with one phone call.

Besides being easy for you, your mother will love the quality and uniqueness of a present from [Great Gifts].

Please review the catalog now! Remember Mother's Day is [May 10].

Thanks in advance for your order.

Sincerely,

[Name]
[Title]

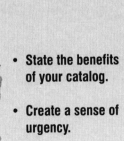

- **State the benefits of your catalog.**

- **Create a sense of urgency.**

Path on CD-ROM: Marketing/Sales→Direct marketing→Announcing a new catalog→Announcing a new catalog—example 1

Asking for a referral

[DATE]

[Name]
[Company]
[Address]
[City, State ZIP]

Dear [   ]:

Thank you for your most recent order, your [fourth] this year. I am very pleased that you are happy with our products and service. You are one of my most valued customers.

Would you do something for me? As a customer of [Plastic Productions], you know you get the best quality and fastest turnaround in town. You also know our prices are competitive and our service excellent. As a business leader, you probably know other companies that could use our service, and your referral would probably carry a lot of weight.

If you make it a policy not to give referrals, I'll understand completely. If you would feel comfortable giving [Plastic Productions] a referral, it would be sincerely appreciated.

I'll call you next week to see what you think. Whatever you decide, I look forward to continuing to work with you.

Sincerely,

[Name]
[Title]

- **Point out the strengths of your company that make it easy to refer you.**

- **Ask for, don't expect, the referral.**

Path on CD-ROM: Marketing/Sales→Direct marketing→Asking for a referral→Asking for a referral—example 1

DIRECT MARKETING

Building store traffic

[DATE]

[Name]
[Company]
[Address]
[City, State ZIP]

Dear [   ]:

It's really true when we say it's the best sale of the year. So don't miss [Summer "Free" Days], when you'll be able to buy one of many items and get another one of the same item absolutely free!

We really appreciate your business and that's why we're offering this great sale opportunity from [3 p.m. to 5 p.m. every Tuesday in May]. In addition to the free items, you'll also [be able to take in a fashion show, meet the author of *Home for the Summer*, and enjoy many pleasant surprises].

Mark your calendar now for these great events. You'll be glad you did.

Sincerely,

[Name]
[Title]

- Make the promotion extend over several weeks to try to bring people in several times.

- Mention the fun and the savings planned for the event.

Path on CD-ROM: Marketing/Sales→Direct marketing→Building store traffic→Building store traffic—example 1

Congratulations on your birthday

[DATE]

[Name]
[Company]
[Address]
[City, State ZIP]

Dear [   ]:

Your birthday is just around the corner. Celebrate by taking your spouse or friend to a romantic dinner for two and the theater at [company].

Bring this letter with you for a 20 percent discount on your dinner and theater tickets. It's our way to say "thank you" for your past patronage and offer you a grand celebration to mark your new year.

Make your reservations today. Choose from the following varied selection of performances:

[1. "The Importance of Being Earnest," Oscar Wilde's masterpiece, runs [date] through [date];]

[2. "A Comedy of Errors," by William Shakespeare, runs [date] through [date];]

[3. "Scrooge," a musical Christmas carol inspired by Charles Dickens, runs [date] through [date].]

This year, select a birthday gift for yourself that you will really enjoy. Make your reservations today. Simply return the enclosed card or phone [(800) 396-3969].

Sincerely,

[Name]
[Title]

- **Personalize your direct mail by tracking dates of importance to your customers.**

- **Offer a choice (which performance, call or mail the order?), but not so many options that they appear daunting to the reader.**

Path on CD-ROM: Marketing/Sales→Direct marketing→Congratulations on birthday→Congratulations on birthday—example 1

DIRECT MARKETING

Congratulations on child's birthday

[DATE]

[Name]
[Company]
[Address]
[City, State ZIP]

Dear [   ]:

Want to do something really different for your child's birthday this year? Give her a no-cost party she will remember for years.

Take your child and her friends to [company's] consumer center. Let them try out a dozen or more of the latest toys on the market and rate them for fun, appeal, and durability.

[We supply the toys and supervision for one and one half hours of toy evaluation time for up to 12 children, age 5-9. Afterward, we supply a party room where you can bring in the birthday cake and juice, and open gifts. We will provide the clean up. For no charge.]

Help us evaluate new toys produced by [company] and our competitors. In the process, give your child a unique birthday experience. Free.

Our schedules fill up fast. Get your reservation in now by calling [777-7777].

Sincerely,

[Name]
[Title]

- **Describe the details of this party service.**

- **Repeat key selling points, for example, "free party."**

Path on CD-ROM: Marketing/Sales→Direct marketing→Congratulations on child's birthday→Congratulations on child's birthday—example 1

Congratulations on your new baby

[DATE]

[Name]
[Company]
[Address]
[City, State ZIP]

Dear [   ]:

A large bird just told us that he delivered a new baby to your house. Congratulations on the addition to your family!

To make caring for your newborn a little easier, we are offering you [two free deliveries from Handy Helper diaper service when you register for a six-month program. You will receive your first two deliveries of fresh, cloth diapers completely free and pay the regular monthly rate for the remainder of the six-month program.]

See for yourself how economical and comfortable [Handy Helper] cloth diapers can be for your infant—and timesaving and hassle-free for you. Also rest assured that cloth diapers are an environmentally friendly alternative to the disposable varieties that clog the county's landfills.

We hope you will take advantage of the this special offer. Just check the program of your choice on the enclosed card and drop it in the mail—no need for a stamp. [We will make your first delivery within three days of receipt of your card.]

Then, you can look forward to regular deliveries of fresh, clean, cloth diapers that are comfortable for your new baby, economical and hassle-free for you, and considerate of the environment.

Best wishes,

[Name]
[Title]

- Letter emphasizes benefits to both parents and their new baby.

- Writer does not spend undue time and space negating the value of disposable diapers; the focus remains on Handy Helper's product.

Path on CD-ROM: Marketing/Sales→Direct marketing→Congratulations on new baby→Congratulations on new baby—example 1

DIRECT MARKETING

Congratulations on your move to a new house

[DATE]

[Name]
[Company]
[Address]
[City, State ZIP]

Dear [   ]:

Welcome to the neighborhood! We just heard about your new home in our area and want to be one of the first to welcome you to the community.

To make your transition a little easier, we are offering you [10 percent off on your first three orders] from [Friendly Grocery, located just down the street at 3333 Brooks Ave. Friendly Grocery] offers the highest quality meats; fresh, locally grown produce in season; and the friendliest staff in town.

We hope you will take advantage of the enclosed coupon and visit [Friendly Grocery] soon. When you come in, please stop by the customer service counter for an additional gift. Then, when you have finished your shopping, just present your coupon at the check-out to receive your [10 percent] discount on all regular and specially priced items.

We are looking forward to meeting you and serving your grocery needs and wants.

Best wishes,

[Name]
[Title]

- **In every paragraph, the focus is on welcoming and serving the newcomer.**

- **Letter provides an extra teaser to the reader in the form of an undisclosed additional gift.**

Path on CD-ROM: Marketing/Sales→Direct marketing→Congratulations on new house→Congratulations on new house—example 1

Congratulations on your promotion letter

[DATE]

[Name]
[Company]
[Address]
[City, State ZIP]

Dear [   ]:

We just heard about your new appointment and would like to join your colleagues in wishing you much success in the years ahead.

To help you reach your goals, we are offering a free two-issue trial subscription to the monthly newsletter, [*Fundraising Alert*]. It covers financial management and resource allocation in higher education.

Recent issues have covered such topics as [how Morris Brown College went from borrowing money to meet the payroll in 1992 to a surplus of nearly $1 million in 1997; why Vassar College began a $206 million fundraising campaign by cutting the budget; and how Villa Julie College and Morgan State University are cooperating to maximize resources].

By informing you about the most effective fundraising and resource allocation strategies at many colleges and universities, [*Fundraising Alert*] multiplies the number of ideas you can test without committing your institution's funds.

To receive your free trial subscription, simply respond by mail, phone, or fax. Then, if you decide to continue your subscription, your cost for [12 more issues is $78, or $68 if you begin your subscription immediately]. This offer expires [DATE].

Let us send you two issues free. Return your response today.

Best wishes in your new appointment,

[Name]
[Editor and Publisher]

- **Promotion begins and ends with a congratulatory note.**

- **Offer provides three ways for the customer to respond.**

Path on CD-ROM: Marketing/Sales→Direct marketing→Congratulations on promotion→Congratulations on promotion—example 1

DIRECT MARKETING

Cover letter

[DATE]

[Name]
[Company]
[Address]
[City, State ZIP]

Dear [   ]:

Your car is one of the most important purchases you make during your life-time. To guarantee that it operates economically and reliably in the months ahead, [Star Motors] is offering a free, diagnostic vehicle check this month to all our customers. It's our way of thanking you for buying your vehicle at [Star Motors]. If our technicians locate any problems requiring repair or adjustment, you will have the option of scheduling your car for servicing.

To take advantage of your free vehicle check, just stop by our service department at [999 State Ave. from 8 a.m. to 5 p.m. Monday through Friday or 8 a.m. to noon on Saturday]. Your free vehicle check will require approximately 20 minutes. While you wait, you may want to stroll through our new car show-room located next to the service department. [When you leave, you will also receive a free Star Motors coffee mug designed to fit snugly into most vehicle cupholders.]

Why wait. Stop by [Star Motors] soon for your free vehicle diagnostic service [and free coffee mug]. Take advantage of the diagnostic service before your next vacation or business trip.

Sincerely,

[Name]
[Title]

- **Letter attracts customers with two different types of free items.**

- **Close reminds readers that they may need the free diagnostic service soon.**

Path on CD-ROM: Marketing/Sales→Direct marketing→Cover letter→Cover letter—example 1

E-mail pitch

[DATE]

[Name]
[Company]
[Address]
[City, State ZIP]

Dear [   ]:

Your purchase of our other wellness publications prompts me to forward to you information on a new book, [*Wellness the Easy Way: 97 Tips for Improved Health*]. The author, [Dr. Miles K. Jones, teaches at [Name] university hospital and explains what he has learned about making healthy living a part of your normal lifestyle—without extra effort].

There is no need to spend your precious dollars and time scouring health food stores or organic food markets. [Dr. Jones provides simple suggestions anyone can use at the grocery store, doctor's office, and even on the job to improve your lifestyle. Dr. Jones addresses questions like "How to prevent weight gain as you get older?" "Do good athletic shoes have to be expensive?" and "Can you control your own blood pressure?"]

[Dr. Jones'] advice can help you stay well and save on all of the costs associated with not operating at your best—including stress and dissatisfaction as well as doctors' bills, prescriptions, and processed foods.

For more information, email [<wellnessdoc@healthscan.com>] or phone [800/888/8888].

- **The e-mail promotion is brief and to the point.**

- **The e-mail message is targeted to people who previously have indicated an interest in this type of product.**

Path on CD-ROM: Marketing/Sales→Direct marketing→E-mail pitch→E-mail pitch—example 1

DIRECT MARKETING

Encouraging a sale from an inactive account

[DATE]

[Name]
[Company]
[Address]
[City, State ZIP]

Dear [   ]:

Your loved ones must be noticing. We are too.

It's been almost [a year] since you ordered flowers for delivery from [Fabulous Flores]. You've been such a good customer that this realization surprised us and prompted us to inquire if there was something we did. If so, we'd like to make amends.

We hope you'll be in touch. In the meantime, mention this letter when you place your next delivery order and we'll take [15 percent off].

Please do call or come in soon. We really appreciate your business.

Sincerely,

[Name]
[Title]

- Use a catchy sales lead.

- Offer a special deal to "jump start" the account.

Path on CD-ROM: Marketing/Sales→Direct marketing→Encouraging a sale from inactive account→Encouraging a sale from inactive account—example 1

Following up after a trade show

[DATE]

[Name]
[Company]
[Address]
[City, State ZIP]

Dear [   ]:

Trade shows are always fun and sometimes the source of information overload. Although I spoke with many people at the recent [IAS] show, I remember that you visited our booth. Thanks for stopping by!

Trade shows are a great time to get a feel for an entire industry. As I stopped at competitors' booths, I realized that [XYW Printers] is the only place you can get [our one-stop services from pre-press to mailing house. When you use our printing services, you're also getting the most experienced printers in town.]

Thanks again for stopping by the booth. It was a pleasure talking with you. For your reference, I've enclosed a brochure about [our new offset printing services].

Sincerely,

[Name]
[Title]

- **Thank the customer or prospect for visiting your trade show booth.**

- **Explain what makes your company stand out from the crowd.**

Path on CD-ROM: Marketing/Sales→Direct marketing→Following up after trade show→Following up after trade show—example 1

DIRECT MARKETING

Following up with a referral

[DATE]

[Name]
[Company]
[Address]
[City, State ZIP]

Dear [   ]:

Have an interest in the best catering services in town?

[Dean Schwartz] suggested you and your firm might be interested in our [sandwich buffet for your monthly staff luncheons]. I have enclosed our menu and brochure for your reference.

I would like to meet with you to see if the [sandwich buffet] or another of our specialty catering services might be of interest to you. I'll give you a call soon to set up a convenient time to meet.

In the meantime, if you have any questions, please call me at [555/555-2834]. I look forward to meeting you.

Thank you for your time.

Sincerely,

[Name]
[Title]

- **Note the name of the person who made the referral.**

- **Name a service the referral might be interested in; show that other services are also available.**

Follow-up

[DATE]

[Name]
[Company]
[Address]
[City, State ZIP]

Dear [   ]:

[Last month] you responded to our advertisement in the [*Wall Street Journal*] about our outdoor trips for professional women, and I sent you brochures about two upcoming trips. I have not heard from you since and wanted to touch base with you once more. I know that busy women cannot always do everything they would like to accomplish and that it's often easiest to put off your own recreation and personal priorities in the face of an overflowing in-basket at the office.

So here is another chance to take advantage of one of our upcoming trips to [northern Minnesota]. It is not too late to register for the [Boundary Waters canoe trip] leaving [August 15 from Grand Marais, Minn., for a week of exploration of the waters and wildlife of this area. This trip is for both experienced and inexperienced paddlers, with two guides and a naturalist to point out features of the terrain, water birds, and other animals.]

A somewhat different experience is set for [Aug. 23–30], when another group leaves from [Grand Marais on a sea kayaking trip on Lake Superior. This trip requires previous kayaking experience.]

Enclosed are brochures covering the details on both of these trips, as well as a list of all trips planned for [August]. If you have questions about any of these trips or would like to reserve your space on one of the above [Minnesota] trips, please write or call [800/999-5555].

I hope you can join us on one of these wonderful wilderness trips.

Sincerely,

[Name]
[Title]

P.S. Don't forget to bring your camera!

- **Introduction contains a positive response to a negative event.**

- **Letter repeats the key elements of the offer.**

Path on CD-ROM: Marketing/Sales→Direct marketing→Follow-up→Follow-up—example 1

DIRECT MARKETING

Force-free trial offer

[DATE]

[Name]
[Company]
[Address]
[City, State ZIP]

Dear [   ]:

Here is your free issue of [magazine], the premier publication on [countryside living in the nation]. Each issue is packed with [how-to articles, timely features, and profiles of individuals who have left city life for their place in the country.]

We are sending you [three] free issues so that you can see for yourself how useful, entertaining, and heart-warming [magazine] can be. Take a few minutes now to skim this first issue. [Learn how one country couple turned their Victorian mansion into a personal spa. Read about the adventure of renewing the beauty of a rippling stream or the pleasures of low-maintenance fruit gardens.]

At the end of your free, [three-issue] subscription, you will have the opportunity to renew at our regular, low subscriber rate, [one-third] less than the newsstand price.

Or, for the best possible rate, order today. Complete and return the enclosed postage-paid card and you will receive [magazine] for an additional year. Of course, you will still receive your [three] free issues.

Sincerely,

[Name]
[Title]

- **Repeat the name of the product and key words, such as "free."**

- **Encourage the reader to order now.**

Path on CD-ROM: Marketing/Sales→Direct marketing→Force-free trial offer→Force-free trial offer—example 1

Helping a sales person out of a slump

INTEROFFICE MEMORANDUM

TO: [   ]
FROM: [   ]
DATE: [   ]
SUBJECT: [Gaining new perspective]

I've noticed that your sales performance has fallen off somewhat in the last few months. I'm surprised and sorry to see that happen to one of our stars.

I know you're thinking about what to do to get back on track, and how you'll rebound in a short time. Psychologists sometimes suggest that when life feels overwhelming that we break it down into smaller pieces. In sales, this translates to setting smaller goals on the path to bigger goals. Are there some smaller goals you can set and achieve that will boost your confidence and get you back on track?

I've always thought you were a particularly talented sales person because you *have a kn*ack with putting people at ease. I'm sure if you focus on this positive characteristic of your style, you'll be able to meet those small goals now, and in a few months, the big ones too.

- **Identify something the sales person does very well.**

- **Make a constructive suggestion.**

Path on CD-ROM: Marketing/Sales→Direct marketing→Helping sales person out of slump→Helping sales person out of slump—example 1

DIRECT MARKETING

Lift letter

A special note from the Editor…

Dear [   ]:

No one knows the challenges of leading today's colleges and universities better than you do. You know only too well the constraints of austere budgets, the pain of financial cutbacks, the low morale of faculty, the worries of students, and the anger of their parents at the high cost of tuition.

Yet you persevere, looking for the answers you know are there, seeking for the seeds of solutions in the heart of the problems.

You have a vision for the success and effectiveness of your institution well into the 21st century.

I want to help you get there.

[*Fundraising Alert*] is designed to extend your network of helpful colleagues at campuses across the globe—without the expense in time or money of traveling to another conference or hiring an outside consultant.

This new publication offers help from those already inside academe, who understand its culture and environment. [*Fundraising Alert*] extends your dialogue on your financial issues with colleagues on other campuses. It extends your range of options when confronting tough situations and offers campus contacts to get more details on what's worked elsewhere.

I invite you to take me up on the charter offer described elsewhere in this package. Experience for yourself the benefits of an expanded collegial network. Use [*Fundraising Alert*] like your personal advisory committee, beginning this fall.

Best wishes,

[Name]
[Editor and Publisher]

- **A lift letter sometimes accompanies a direct mail package and provides an additional teaser to the reader. Often, it begins, "Open this only if you have decided not to order."**

- **This lift letter provides a more personal reason to purchase the product.**

Path on CD-ROM: Marketing/Sales→Direct marketing→Lift letter→Lift letter—example 1

Magazine ad lead

[DATE]

[Name]
[Company]
[Address]
[City, State ZIP]

Dear [   ]:

Thank you for your response to our advertisement in the [*Wall Street Journal*]. Our outdoor trips for women offer busy professionals like yourself an opportunity to relax while enriching your life through camping, hiking, skiing, snowshoeing, canoeing, and kayaking experiences across the U.S.

You indicated that you want to take a vacation in [August] and have always wanted to explore the [Boundary Waters Canoe Area of northern Minnesota]. We have a [canoe trip scheduled for August 15 through 22 in cooperation with Grand Marais Outfitters that would give you an entire week to explore the waters and wildlife of this area. This trip is for both experienced and inexperienced paddlers, with two guides and a naturalist to point out features of the terrain, water birds, and other animals.]

A somewhat different experience is set for [Aug. 23–30], when another group leaves from [Grand Marais on a sea kayaking trip on Lake Superior]. This trip requires previous kayaking experience.

Enclosed are brochures covering the details on both of these trips, as well as a list of all trips planned for [August]. If you have questions about any of these trips or would like to reserve your space on one of the above [Minnesota] trips, please write or call [800/999-5555].

I appreciate your interest in outdoor trips for women.

Regards,

[Name]
[Title]

P.S. I am looking forward to meeting you on one of our canoeing or kayaking journeys soon.

- **The letter zeroes in on the customer's specific interest areas.**

- **The postscript personalizes the communication.**

Path on CD-ROM: Marketing/Sales→Direct marketing→Magazine ad lead→Magazine ad lead—example 1

DIRECT MARKETING

Post card

[DATE]

[Name]
[Company]
[Address]
[City, State ZIP]

Dear [   ]:

[Find your place in the country without leaving your living room.]

Did you know that you can enjoy our [rural living] magazine without the bother of picking it up at your newsstand? [And that you can save 35 percent in the process?]

Complete and return this card to begin your 12-month subscription to [magazine] at less than you would pay for a good dinner out with your partner. [Enjoy a dozen issues for less than the price of eight.]

We will begin your subscription as soon as we receive your card and invoice you after the first issue.

Sign me up! Begin my 12-month subscription to [magazine] immediately. I understand that you will send an invoice for [sum] after I have received my first issue.

Name _____

Address _____

City _____ State _____ ZIP _____

- **Insert a post card/response sheet into your publication or other product to attract new or more frequent customers.**

- **In the short space available, emphasize the primary benefits to the customer: price and convenience.**

Path on CD-ROM: Marketing/Sales→Direct marketing→Post card→Post card—example 1

Renewal letter

[DATE]

[Name]
[Company]
[Address]
[City, State ZIP]

Dear [   ]:

Stretch your budget dollars. Renew your 12-month subscription to [magazine] now and receive a FREE issue (13 issues for the price of 12).

Save time, money, and paperwork later by extending your subscription to [magazine] now.

Your subscription to [magazine] will end on [date]. To ensure that you continue to receive every issue of your valuable subscription at the best possible rate, please return the enclosed renewal certificate today. Take advantage of the special, FREE issue offer.

Sincerely,

[Name]
[Title]

- Offer a great deal for renewing early, which saves you the cost of additional mailings.

- Include a premium or extra issues as an additional incentive.

Path on CD-ROM: Marketing/Sales→Direct marketing→Renewal letter→Renewal letter—example 1

DIRECT MARKETING

Requesting names of clients to invite to a trade show

INTEROFFICE MEMORANDUM

TO: [Company Sales Staffers]
FROM: [   ]
DATE: [   ]
SUBJECT: [Trade show guest list]

Looking for ways to strengthen your client relationships? Invite them to visit the [Sample Company] booth at the [IAS] trade show next month—and plan to attend yourself!

Please provide me with a list of the names and addresses of clients you would like to invite to the trade show, noting what could be gained by the attendance of each.

To get the invitations out in time, I'll need to have your list in hand no later than [May 2]. A future memo will advise about which of your customers have been invited.

Mark your calendar. The trade show will be held [June 28–30 at the convention center]. Our booth number is [332].

- **Set a deadline for when you need the names.**

- **Expect the sales people to attend the trade show as well.**

Path on CD-ROM: Marketing/Sales→Direct marketing→Requesting names of clients to invite to trade show→Requesting names of clients to invite to trade show—example 1

Response sheet/order form

[*Fundraising Alert*] Charter Subscription

__ Yes, please start my charter subscription to [*Fundraising Alert* for only $99. Send my first two issues for FREE. If I subscribe, I'll receive 14 issues for the price of 12]. If I decide not to subscribe, I'll write cancel on the invoice and the [two free issues] are mine to keep.

__ Please bill me/my institution for [$99].

__ I like the idea of saving [$10] right away. Enclosed is payment information to start my subscription. [I'll receive 14 issues for the price of 12]. If at the end of the year I feel I didn't get my money's worth, I'll request my refund.

__ Charge my   __ MC __ VISA   Card # _____   Exp _____

Signature_____

__ Check for [$89] is enclosed.

For immediate service, call toll free [800/999-9999] or fax your order to [800/888-8888].

This offer expires on [DATE].

- **Response sheet encourages immediate action with a discounted price for a decision now.**

- **An expiration date also emphasizes the importance of responding now.**

Path on CD-ROM: Marketing/Sales→Direct marketing→Response sheet→Response sheet—example 1

Soliciting a sale from a long-term inactive account

[DATE]

[Name]
[Company]
[Address]
[City, State ZIP]

Dear [   ]:

We're getting the message you no longer want to hear from us!

We worked together so well for many years, and now it's been a long time since we've had an order from you. Was it something we did? If so, we'd like to try to make it up to you. We'd also like to continue to provide you with the [high quality ball bearings you were so pleased with in the past].

Before giving up, we wanted to at least write to you and see if there was anything we could do to win back your business. Please let us know.

We look forward to hearing from you.

Sincerely,

[Name]
[Title]

- **Talk about previous positive working relationship.**

- **Try to find out what has changed in the business relationship.**

Path on CD-ROM: Marketing/Sales→Direct marketing→Soliciting sale from long-term inactive account→Soliciting sale from long-term inactive account—example 1

Telemarketing script

Hello. This is [Name] calling about your subscription to [*Fundraising Alert*].

Your subscription is ending soon, and we want to make sure that it has met your needs.

Has your copy of [*Fundraising Alert*] arrived promptly each month?

What kinds of [fundraising] topics are of most interest to you?

Do you plan to renew your subscription to [*Fundraising Alert*]?

A) IF THE RESPONSE IS "NO," SAY: May I ask why not?

FOLLOWED BY: Is there someone else in your organization who may better benefit from a subscription to [*Fundraising Alert*]?

CLOSE: Thank you for your time and honest comments.

B) IF THE RESPONSE IS "YES," SAY: Would you like to renew your subscription now? We can bill you at a later date and you will ensure that your subscription to [*Fundraising Alert*] will continue uninterrupted.

CLOSE: Thank you for your thoughtful comments and subscription renewal.

- **This letter ensures that the customer understands that his feedback about the product is important.**

- **Even a negative response can garner useful information for the publisher/ business owner.**

Path on CD-ROM: Marketing/Sales→Direct marketing→Telemarketing script→Telemarketing script—example 1

DIRECT MARKETING

Thanking for a referral

[DATE]

[Name]
[Company]
[Address]
[City, State ZIP]

Dear [   ]:

Thanks for recommending [my law firm to Mike Thom], and for providing me with his phone number.

[Mike] and I spoke on [Friday afternoon] and hit it off well. I am confident that we will be doing business sometime in the near future.

Because you had said such complimentary things about our services, [Mike] was already enthusiastic about working with us when I called. Thank you for thinking of our firm and for your personal recommendation.

Sincerely,

[Name]
[Title]

- **Explain how the referral is panning out.**

- **Show your appreciation for the referral.**

Path on CD-ROM: Marketing/Sales→Direct marketing→Thanking for a referral→Thanking for a referral—example 1

Trade show lead

[DATE]

[Name]
[Company]
[Address]
[City, State ZIP]

Dear [   ]:

I enjoyed meeting you last week at the [National Cheese Makers Expo] and learning about your business. You mentioned that [international demand for whey products seemed to be up and this might be a good year for your company to begin selling globally.]

[You were right. When I got back to the office, I checked with the U.S. Department of Agriculture, and international sales for whey products have increased dramatically over the past two years.]

[Company] can put you in touch with overseas markets through our extensive network of affiliated representatives in [16] countries. We can also help tailor your promotional messages to manufacturers and business leaders in these nations.

You may be interested in an upcoming [international marketing conference we are sponsoring in Jakarta, Indonesia, two months from now]. It could offer you the [introductory contacts into the Asian marketplace that you are looking for].

If you would like to attend the [Jakarta] conference or [work with our representative in a specific country], please give me a call. [Company] would appreciate the opportunity of helping you launch the export side of your business.

Sincerely,

[Name]
[Title]

- **Writer specifies how and when she met the trade show customer.**

- **This letter indicates how the writer has already begun to serve the potential customer — through tracking down needed information.**

Path on CD-ROM: Marketing/Sales→Direct marketing→Trade show lead→Trade show lead—example 1

DIRECT MARKETING

Welcome letter

[DATE]

[Name]
[Company]
[Address]
[City, State ZIP]

Dear [   ]:

Welcome to the best available network in higher education! Your subscription to [newsletter] links you to the most innovative ideas and strategies that your peers around the globe have discovered.

You can turn to [newsletter] to spark your brainstorming sessions and motivate your harried staff. Route your issue to key decision makers on your campus. Borrow its ideas to solve problems and improve the academy.

[newsletter] is your voice in higher education. Whenever you have a solution to share, a new program to announce or any other success story, we would like to hear about it. Our best editorial ideas come from our readers.

Whenever you have a suggestion or tip to share, please call our editorial hotline, [(800) 999-8888]. With your help, each issue of [newsletter] will be better than the one before.

Sincerely,

[Name]
[Title]

- **Suggest additional uses for the product.**

- **Encourage interaction with the company, product or service. Work to build future repeat business.**

Path on CD-ROM: Marketing/Sales→Direct marketing→Welcome letter→Welcome letter—example 1

Questionnaires/surveys

Getting real feedback can be the sales person's dream. Numbers can show what customers want—and what makes them buy. Good numbers are difficult to come by, however, and survey design is quite complicated.

Several strategies can help generate responses to questionnaires or surveys. A good cover letter can use sales techniques to draw the reader in. Asking for help, using a catchy lead-in paragraph, using a pretty stamp, gentle flattery, and enclosing a dollar are all strategies that can boost responses. Suggesting that the survey will be easy to complete and return can also help.

In general, open-ended questions (which don't suggest a response) are asked first, followed by a series of closed-ended questions (which suggest a response through multiple choice, true/false, or other means.)

Some surveys don't need to be sophisticated to be effective, as long as you don't want statistically significant results. For example, a very simple survey within a letter may be just enough to get a prospect thinking about what he or she needs—and how what you're selling might help.

You can use the sample cover letters and questionnaires as excellent starting points. If you want truly statistically valid data, however, consider hiring the help of a professional in this area. Survey design for highly accurate results is beyond the scope of this book.

Accompanying a questionnaire

[DATE]

[Name]
[Company]
[Address]
[City, State ZIP]

Dear [   ]:

We really enjoyed serving you and, even though we no longer directly do business, we value your opinion.

Would you help us improve our products and services by completing the enclosed questionnaire? It is important that the survey be completed by the person most responsible for decisions affecting the purchase of [product]. It will only take a few moments, and we would be most obliged if you would return it in the provided self-addressed stamped envelope by [date].

Thank you very much.

Sincerely,

[Name]
[Title]

- **Open with gentle compliments.**

- **Use a response-increasing strategy, such as asking for help.**

Path on CD-ROM: Marketing/Sales→Questionnaires-surveys→Accompanying questionnaire→Accompanying questionnaire—example 1

Informing of survey results

[DATE]

[Name]
[Company]
[Address]
[City, State ZIP]

Dear [   ]:

Thank you so much for completing our recent [industry] industry compensation survey. Surprisingly, salaries for many positions have not increased as much as expected. The full survey results have been compiled into [company]'s annual Compensation Report.

This data-packed product has been a relied-upon source of compensation data for the [industry] industry for more than a decade. This year's manual is available to non-participants for $[amount]. As a survey participant, you may purchase it for the special discounted price of $[amount].

As a special token of our appreciation, please find enclosed a gift certificate for an additional $[amount] off when you order your copy of the survey results before [date].

Thanks again for helping us improve our products and services. We look forward to your feedback on the report.

Sincerely,

[Name]
[Title]

- **Use a salient survey result to sell the whole report.**

- **Say thank you in several ways, including providing participants with special discounts.**

Path on CD-ROM: Marketing/Sales→Questionnaires-surveys→Informing of survey results→Informing of survey results—example 1

163

Surveying customers

Thank you for answering the following questions. Please return your questionnaire in the enclosed self-addressed stamped envelope by [date].

Please list the top three reasons you do business with [company].
1.
2.
3.

Over the past year how often have you ordered from [company]? (Please circle one)
a) 0
b) 1-5
c) 6-9
d) 10 or more

Overall how would you rate your satisfaction with [company]'s products you have received? (Please circle one)
a) very satisfied
b) somewhat satisfied
c) somewhat dissatisfied
d) very dissatisfied

Overall how would you rate your satisfaction with [company]'s service? (Please circle one)
a) very satisfied
b) somewhat satisfied
c) somewhat dissatisfied
d) very dissatisfied

OPTIONAL:

Name
Company
Phone number

Thank you for taking the time to answer these questions!

- **Ask mostly closed-end questions (i.e., multiple choice or true-false).**

- **Thank the person for participating and provide information on what to do with the completed survey.**

Path on CD-ROM: Marketing/Sales→Questionnaires-surveys→Surveying customers→Surveying customers—example 1

Surveying potential customers

Thank you for answering the following questions. Please return your questionnaire in the enclosed self-addressed stamped envelope by [date].

What are the top three reasons you buy [product]?
1.
2.
3.

Over the past year, how often have you ordered [products]? (Please circle one)
a) 0
b) 1-5
c) 6-9
d) 10 or more

Overall how would you rate your satisfaction with your supplier's products? (Please circle one)
a) very satisfied
b) somewhat satisfied
c) somewhat dissatisfied
d) very dissatisfied

Overall how would you rate your satisfaction with your supplier's service? (Please circle one)
a) very satisfied
b) somewhat satisfied
c) somewhat dissatisfied
d) very dissatisfied

What is the main reason you do business with your [product] supplier?

Who is your [product] supplier?

OPTIONAL:
Name
Company
Phone number

Thank you for taking the time to answer these questions!

- **Ask mostly closed-end questions (i.e., multiple choice or true-false).**

- **Thank the person for participating and provide information on what to do with the completed survey.**

Path on CD-ROM: Marketing/Sales→Questionnaires-surveys→Surveying potential customers→Surveying potential customers—example 1

165

QUESTIONNAIRES/SURVEYS

Thanking for completing a questionnaire

[DATE]

[Name]
[Company]
[Address]
[City, State ZIP]

Dear [   ]:

Thank you so much for completing our recent survey questionnaire. We value your opinions very much and will definitely be taking action on the results of the survey.

As a special token of our appreciation, please find enclosed a [gift certificate, coupon, other giveaway].

Thanks again for helping us improve our products and services.

Sincerely,

[Name]
[Title]

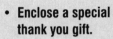

- **Enclose a special thank you gift.**

- **Say that the respondent's opinions are valuable.**

Path on CD-ROM: Marketing/Sales→Questionnaires-surveys→Thanking for completing questionnaire→Thanking for completing questionnaire—example 1

Management

Managing is much like piloting a boat. Both require forward thrust and a delicate sense of balance—attuned to the needs of diverse constituencies. Despite internal challenges and the wind and waves of external factors attempting to drive you off course, you must maintain your compass setting.

Whether you are communicating with employees, shareholders, customers, vendors, or other groups, you must know when to "go with the flow" and when to "stay the course." In other words, management is as much art as science. Still, there are maps and channel markers to guide you on your way. For instance, consider the following pointers:

- Take initiative. When you glimpse a potential opportunity, move toward it.
- Be flexible. When the wind begins to shift or the motor sounds sluggish, maneuver accordingly. Expect the unexpected. Do not become bound by the rules. Know that there is no typical day.
- Be open. Share facts and delegate problems. Allow people to help your company move toward its goals.
- Explain what you want to happen. Repeat your expectations and goals. Again. And again.
- Be positive. Do not operate out of doubt. Expect the response you want. Remember that employees and other people want to do the right thing.
- Be direct. Confront problems and opportunities equally. Do not hide.
- Express appreciation to employees, customers, shareholders, vendors, and others who help the company grow and fulfill its goals.

Announcements—annual report

[DATE]

[Name/Title]
[Business/Organization Name]
[Address]
[City, State ZIP]

Dear Chairman [   ]:

We will release our annual report within the week, but I wanted to reach you first with our good news. Not only has the firm reached its projected budget increases of [6.3 percent] in all categories, but several categories have surpassed their goals by as much as [3 percent]. This means corporate performance has not only improved but, in light of the current financial climate facing our industry, exceeded our most optimistic expectations.

Specifically, overall revenues in all categories met or only slightly missed budgeted goals. The greatest disparity was [less than 3 percent]. In several categories—[notably electronic applications, bulk distribution, and specialty services]—performance exceeded budget by [1.3 percent to 4.9 percent]. Our average overall revenue increase totaled [7.2 percent], or [0.9 percent]more than budget.

Operational cost savings also exceeded expectations. If you will recall, we had projected cost reductions totaling 18 percent compared to last year's operational budget. While some categories varied, our overall reduction totaled 23 percent, or 5 percent more than the budgeted amount.

Chief Financial Officer [Jeffrey Toole] will brief the entire board on all details at this month's meeting. But I chose to exercise my right as chief executive officer to share the good news with you first. I know [Jeff] won't mind.

If you have any questions, please feel free to call either [Jeff] or me. Otherwise, we look forward to a productive board meeting and a prosperous new year.

Best regards,

[Name]
[Title]

- **Start off with the good news.**

- **Summarize your accomplishments.**

Path on CD-ROM: Management→Announcements→Annual report→Annual report—example 1

Apology—employee

To: [EMPLOYEE]
From: [NAME]
Date: [   ]
Subject: [   ]

I'm sorry that I missed our appointment early this morning. I inadvertently scheduled a breakfast meeting outside the office for the same time that we were to meet and did not check my office calendar before driving across town.

Maybe we can get together for lunch later this week? I have reviewed your proposal for [launching a new product line of door hardware for home remodelers and think that it might strengthen our market position with this group]. I would like to discuss your proposal in depth with you. Please let me know if you are available for lunch on [Thursday or Friday].

- **Putting the apology at the top of this memo gets the reader's immediate and positive attention.**

- **Going the extra mile by offering to meet for lunch as soon as convenient strengthens the apology.**

Path on CD-ROM: Management→Apology→Employee→Employee—example 1

Award—company

INTEROFFICE MEMORANDUM

TO: [   ]
FROM: [   ]
DATE: [   ]
SUBJECT: [Old Shaker Furniture nominated for Humanitarian Award]

[The Old Shaker Furniture Co.] believes that aiding one's fellow man is a moral imperative in today's society. That belief translates in the way we do business.

When [Home and Garden Furniture] was destroyed by a fire last month, we could have sat back and let the employees deal with the problem. Instead, we offered [John Hammer, H&G Furniture's CEO], space in our warehouse to rebuild his company. Some would say that we were foolish for sharing our company's space with a competitor. We believe it was the moral thing to do.

It seems that others thought our decision was right. We just received word that we were nominated for the [Alger Humanitarian Award]. [Give some background information about the award.]

The winner of the [Alger Humanitarian Award will be announced next month at a dinner in Manhattan].

- **Announce the award and describe award's importance.**

- **Reiterate company's philosophy.**

Path on CD-ROM: Management→Award→Company→Company—example 1

Award—individual

INTEROFFICE MEMO

TO: [   ]
FROM: [   ]
DATE: [   ]
SUBJECT: [Judith Richards nominated for CEO of the Year]

[The Businesswomen's Club of Greater Nashville] has nominated [ChainLink Industries' CEO, Judith Richards], for CEO of the Year.

Each year, the [Businesswomen's Club] nominates candidates who they believe personify the positive characteristics of a corporate CEO. Nominees must exhibit success in the workplace as well as volunteer activities.

In addition to leading [ChainLink Industries] toward record profits, [Ms. Richards] also finds time to serve on the boards of several nonprofit organizations including the [Nashville Girl Guides and the Baker Hospital].

The CEO of the Year will be announced at the [Businesswomen's Club annual meeting on December 18th].

- Announce nomination and describe award's importance.

- Explain why individual was nominated.

Path on CD-ROM: Management→Award→Individual→Individual—example 1

Bad news—company sale

INTEROFFICE MEMORANDUM

TO: [ALL EMPLOYEES]
FROM: [NAME]
DATE: [   ]
SUBJECT: [   ]

[Eastern Ridge Community Bank] has served individual and business customers in our region for many years and always has earned a profit for shareholders. Most of our shareholders have owned bank stock for years, in some cases even inheriting it from the preceding generation. Many shareholders and directors now have reached retirement age.

At a meeting last night they voted to accept an offer to sell this bank to [Constitutional Community Bancorporation]. The sale, of course, is pending regulatory approval. We expect it to be finalized by mid year.

[Constitutional Community] is well known nationally for a policy of permitting its banks to operate independently, retaining local boards of directors and management. Except for the change in ownership, little else about the bank will change in the near future.

[Eastern Ridge] likely will take advantage of [Constitutional Community's] data processing and other centralized services instead of outsourcing these to other state vendors. Our staff, products, and services, however, will remain virtually unchanged.

- **First paragraph sets the scene for explaining the sale.**

- **What is unstated is often as important as what is stated. Managers are sometimes tempted to close by offering to answer questions about an event. But the offer can suggest uncertainty or that information has been hidden, when in truth all of the key facts have been presented.**

Path on CD-ROM: Management→Bad news→Company sale→Company sale—example1

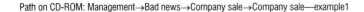

Bad news—layoffs

INTEROFFICE MEMORANDUM

TO: [   ]
FROM: [   ]
DATE: [   ]
SUBJECT: [   ]

Times are changing. Many of us can remember when the main product of our company was [boat trailers]. Of course, [navigational instruments have comprised 90] percent of our business for the past [decade]. At the last board meeting, our directors voted to close our [boat trailer facility in Bolton Junction] and focus all of our resources on our growing [instrumentation divisions].

The [trailer facility] will close on [August 30]. Each of the [53] employees will receive a generous severance package, including career counseling, six months salary, and benefits. Any employees desiring to transfer here to [Grand Harbor] will be considered for openings as they occur.

Department heads who expect to have position openings in the next six months may send job descriptions to the human resources office to match with [Bolton Junction] candidates.

- **Historical context makes the layoffs understandable.**

- **Message offers glimmer of hope to laid-off workers in the form of a severance package and job prospects at the company's headquarters.**

Path on CD-ROM: Management→Bad news→Layoffs→Layoffs—example 1

Celebrations—anniversary dates outside company

[DATE]

[Name/Title]
[Business/Organization Name]
[Address]
[City, State ZIP]

Dear [   ]:

It is our distinct pleasure to commend and recognize [*complete name of firm*] on its [*name of achievement or number of anniversary*]. Under your leadership, your firm's contributions to the industry have been many. Despite the challenges facing today's [*name of product*] providers, [*shortened name of firm*] has long been known for its outstanding performance and service.

[**Optional paragraph 1:** *Outline recent corporate achievements, using two to three examples to draw a single conclusion of excellent performance or outstanding service.*]

[**Optional paragraph 2:** *Outline superior individual performance or corporate performance under the leadership of the letter's recipient. Follow the same approach used in Optional Paragraph 1.*]

We recognize the continued challenges facing the [*name of industry*] industry. We have no doubt that [*name of firm*] will continue to excel in providing America's demanding consumers with excellence in both products and service.

Our hats are off to you. Best of luck carving new [*shortened name of industry*] industry frontiers in the future.

Sincerely,

[Name]
[Title]

- **List specific reasons why the firm or individual deserves the praise.**

- **Wish them future good fortune.**

Path on CD-ROM: Management→Celebrations→Anniversary dates outside company→Anniversary dates outside company—example 1

Celebrations—individual

INTEROFFICE MEMO

TO: [   ]
FROM: [   ]
DATE: [   ]
SUBJECT: [Kudos for handling a difficult situation well]

When faced with a situation like the one you faced yesterday, most individuals would have let the customer walk away and lose the account. When [George Rogers was berating you about his late deliveries], your demeanor and ability to empathize allowed [George] to save face when we discovered the problem wasn't with our company. Your willingness to work with [George] saved our account with [Rogers, Inc.]

Thank you for your persistence and patience on that difficult account.

I want to celebrate your efforts and buy you lunch at the [Fisheries Restaurant]. I have reserved [Friday, April 12th] on my calendar. Please check your calendar and let me know if that is a good date for you.

Once again, I appreciate your efforts in going the extra mile.

- **Memo describes the behavior that earned the written praise and a lunch.**

- **Writer expresses congratulations for handling a difficult situation.**

Path on CD-ROM: Management→Celebrations→Individual→Individual—example 2

Complaints—manager to subordinate

INTEROFFICE MEMORANDUM

TO: [   ]
FROM: [   ]
DATE: [   ]
SUBJECT: [Adhering to scheduled work hours]

[Bryce], your inability to get down to business at 8:00 a.m. is causing us to lose customer calls. Frequently you are seen drinking coffee and chatting with colleagues in other departments rather than sitting at your workstation answering incoming calls. This behavior means that our limited staff is forced to handle your calls. The lines become clogged and customers get tired of waiting on hold. This leads to missing customer calls.

[Bryce], we need everyone ready to work at 8:00 a.m. If you like to start your day by chatting with colleagues, I suggest you arrive at 7:30 a.m.

I expect that tomorrow and on future days I will see you at your workstation with your headset on, ready to take calls promptly at 8:00 a.m.

- **Describe the problem.**

- **Explain how you want the problem to be solved.**

Path on CD-ROM: Management→Complaints→Manager to subordinate→Manager to subordinate—example 1

Compliments—enjoyed article

[DATE]

[Name]
[Address]
[City, State ZIP]

Dear [   ]:

Imagine my surprise when I opened your letter and discovered a copy of the article that I was having trouble locating. Thank you for you sending it to me.

As we had discussed at the meeting on [Wednesday], the principles included in the article are very relevant to the current business climate. The author offers several suggestions that may be useful for one of our upcoming projects, which is why I wanted to locate a copy of it.

Thank you again for remembering my interest in the article.

Sincerely,

[Name]
[Title]

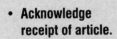

- **Acknowledge receipt of article.**

- **Thank the sender for his/her thoughtfulness.**

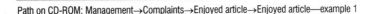

Path on CD-ROM: Management→Complaints→Enjoyed article→Enjoyed article—example 1

Deals—calling off decision/action

[DATE]

[Name]
[Company]
[Address]
[City, State ZIP]

Dear [   ]:

I enjoyed finally meeting you personally last week after so many weeks of communicating by correspondence and telephone calls.

The process of planning for the sale of [our family of healthcare newsletters] has taught me much about the value and potential of this product line. I regret to inform you that I have decided not to sell [these newsletters] after all.

If I ever decide to sell them in the years ahead, you will be the first publisher that I contact.

Sincerely,

[Name]
[Title]

- **Buffer the bad news with a positive or neutral beginning and ending.**

- **Clearly explain that plans have changed.**

Path on CD-ROM: Management→Deals→Calling off decision-action→Calling off decision-action—example 1

Deals—encouraging decision/action

[DATE]

[Name]
[Company]
[Address]
[City, State ZIP]

Dear [   ]:

I enjoyed meeting with you [two weeks] ago and learning about your plans to expand your [flower and gift shop] business. When we toured my [Main Street] property, you indicated that it seemed like the right location for your growing business.

Since we met, I have received several inquiries as to the availability of the [Main Street] property for lease. While I am eager to lease the property, which now has stood vacant for [two months], I would like to give you the opportunity of first refusal. You are right that it would be a good location for a [flower and gift shop]. (The other interested parties propose using the space for a [photography studio, insurance agency, and other professional offices].)

If you are still interested in leasing the [Main Street] building, please call me soon. I hope that we reach a win-win agreement, enabling your [flower and gift shop] to expand to [Main Street].

Sincerely,

[Name]
[Title]

- **First paragraph explains what has prompted concern.**

- **Last paragraph extends a hope for a mutually agreeable outcome.**

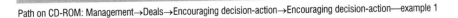

Path on CD-ROM: Management→Deals→Encouraging decision-action→Encoderaging decision-action—example 1

Decline to do business

[DATE]

[Name]
[Company]
[Address]
[City, State ZIP]

Dear [   ]:

Thank you for contacting us regarding our facilities.

In your letter of [date] you inquired about the availability of our facilities for hosting [event] on [date 2] for [number] of people. We have regularly hosted groups as large or larger than the numbers you are describing. However, on [date 2], our [room] will be closed for remodeling. Our next biggest room will hold only [number 2] of people.

We regret that we will not be able to serve your group this year. May I recommend that you contact the [company]? I know they have previously served groups your size or larger.

Good luck on your [event] and please consider us for future [events].

Sincerely,

[Name]
[Title]

- **Acknowledge the request and explain the reason for the refusal.**

- **Suggest an alternative, if appropriate.**

Path on CD-ROM: Management→Miscellaneous→Decline to do business→Decline to do business—example 2

Decline to do business—prior commitment

[DATE]

[Name]
[Company]
[Address]
[City, State ZIP]

Dear [   ]:

Thank you for your interest in supplying us with legal representation. We have reviewed your vita and proposal and found them both to be quite impressive. Your firm's experience in [intellectual property litigation] is quite considerable.

We are, however, quite pleased with the representation we receive from [Long, Jones, and Howard]. The attorneys we work with there have a combined total of [60 years] of experience in [intellectual property law] and have represented us for [over 20 years]. At this point, we are not interested in making a change.

Thank you for your interest in doing business with [JAK Publishing Company].

Sincerely,

[Name]
[Title]

- **Acknowledge receipt of documents.**

- **Decline proposal and explain why.**

Path on CD-ROM: Management→Decline business→Prior commitment→Prior commitment—example 1

Events—invitation

[DATE]

[Name/Title]
[Business/Organization Name]
[Address]
[City, State ZIP]

Dear [   ]:

The [State Street Emporium] is growing in its service to [metropolitan Dade County]. We have planned a gala celebration and open house to commemorate our success and set our sights on future growth.

Won't you [chase away the blues of income tax season and] join us [Saturday, April 16] for [champagne, caviar, and dancing to the music of Jimmy Changa and his Salsa Allstars]? The open house will run from [5 p.m. until 10 p.m.]

Bring your [dancing shoes and your favorite partner]. We'll take care of the rest.

Cheers,

[Name]
[Title]

- **Explain the cause for the celebration.**

- **Mention the time, date, and place.**

Path on CD-ROM: Management→Events→Invitation→Invitation—example 1

Events—merger

[DATE]

[Name/Title]
[Business/Organization Name]
[Address]
[City, State ZIP]

Dear [   ]:

This letter serves as formal notice to you as chairman and to the rest of the board that the National Credit Union Administration has directed that the assets and members of [Cloverleaf Federal Credit Union] be merged with those of [Deep Woods Federal Credit Union], effective [November 1]. You have been notified orally by administration representatives, and they will be following up with their own written notification shortly.

In the administration's eyes, this merger is necessary for the safety and protection of both credit union members' funds, and the industry's insurance fund. The board of [Cloverleaf Federal Credit Union] will be retained in an advisory capacity for six months beginning [October 1] to help effect a smooth merger.

The administration recognizes and appreciates the assistance you and your fellow directors have provided in facilitating this merger, and holds none of you accountable for the tenuous financial condition into which [Cloverleaf] fell after the closing of its primary sponsor, [Blacktop Industries].

As chairman of [Deep Woods Federal Credit Union], I look forward to working with you to protect the assets of your members. We appreciate your contributions, both now and over the next few months, and know our merger efforts will be successful.

Sincerely,

[Name]
[Title]

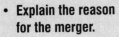

- **Explain the reason for the merger.**

- **Make sure it's clear that you're not placing any blame on the recipient of the letter.**

Path on CD-ROM: Management→Events→Merger→Merger—example 1

Events—resignation

MEMORANDUM

TO: [President]
FROM: [   ]
DATE: [   ]

After ten years of learning much and working hard to further the goals of this organization, I find that I am now ready to move down another path. It is with a mixture of both happiness and regret that I tender my resignation to this organization.

Certain periods of our lives are rich with experiences and opportunities. That is how the last ten years here have been. All that I have gained and have been allowed to put into practice has been noticed by a major corporation, which has offered me significant new opportunities to grow and prosper. It is something I simply cannot afford to pass up.

I offer my heartfelt thanks to those in the company who have encouraged my professional development and provided support for my initiatives over the years. I have gained a great deal from working here, and I hope I have been able to return a least part of what I have gained in loyalty and value to the firm.

- **Explain how you're leaving with a positive attitude.**

- **Thank the old firm.**

Path on CD-ROM: Management→Events→Resign→Resign—example 1

FYI—informing subordinates with pleasure

INTEROFFICE MEMORANDUM

TO: [   ]
FROM: [   ]
DATE: [   ]
SUBJECT: Scheduling Change

After much discussion and the recommendation of the staff supervisors, the executive committee has agreed to change the schedule for all [resident care-givers]. Starting [July 1], [caregivers] will only be required to work every other weekend instead of two out of every three weekends.

This change will give our dedicated staff an additional weekend per month off. New schedules will be posted [by the nurses' stations on each wing].

- **Announce the good news.**

- **Explain how the news will affect employees.**

Path on CD-ROM: Management→FYI→Informing subordinates pleasure→Informing subordinates pleasure—example 3

M E M O R A N D U M

TO: [Vice President of Public Relations]
FROM: [Accounting]
DATE: [   ]
SUBJECT: [Client Spending]

It has come to our attention that your department and you in particular spend an inordinate amount of time and money entertaining out-of-town clients. We understand that this is your job, and we appreciate your work on behalf of all of us at this company. But we note that at this rate, you will exceed your entertainment budget for the year by at least 25 percent.

We would like to make a suggestion. Since much of this entertaining is done by you along with various department heads, may we suggest that those department heads be allowed to pick up a certain percentage of the tabs when discussions are germane to their business, and include it as part of their T&E expense for the project being discussed. In this way, everyone will stay within budget. It also will look less imposing to accountants and auditors than if the full amount were listed on one credit card.

We offer this suggestion in the best interest of the company and hope you will take it as such. Thank you for your consideration.

- **Express an appreciation for their responsibilities.**

- **Offer a creative solution.**

Goodwill—acknowledging request for a donation

[DATE]

[Name]
[Address]
[City, State ZIP]

Dear [   ]:

Thank you for your letter of [date] requesting a donation to [event].

Our company policy states that all charitable requests must be routed to the [name] committee for approval. The [name] committee meets monthly to review any requests and approve disbursements.

I have passed your letter along to the head of the [name] committee. It will be reviewed [next month] and you should get a response after [date].

In the meantime, I wish you success in your fundraising efforts.

Sincerely,

[Name]
[Title]

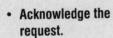

- **Acknowledge the request.**

- **Explain company policy regarding donations.**

Path on CD-ROM: Management→Goodwill→Acknowledging request for donation→Acknowledging request for donation—example 4

Goodwill—seeking more information

[DATE]

[Name/Title]
[Business/Organization Name]
[Address]
[City, State ZIP]

Dear [   ]:

I received your letter asking for permission to use my name in your upcoming fundraising efforts. I also have thoroughly familiarized myself with the [*name of company/foundation*]. Of all the charities that seek my assistance or support, few have worked as hard with as little or have done as much as your organization. I am impressed with your past successes.

Before I give you approval to use my name, however, I need to know more about the focus of this campaign and how and to whom its funds will be disbursed. I also would like to see and have my attorney review the letter as well as establish limits and guidelines on how the letter may be used.

In years past, I've known executives like me who have lent their names to sloppy and/or unscrupulous charities and have wound up facing lawsuits as a result. I have every wish to assist your efforts, but I think both our needs will be best served if we establish some boundaries.

Feel free to contact my assistant, [*name*], to set up an appointment. I look forward to meeting with you and discovering how I can assist the [*name of company/foundation*].

Best regards,

[Name]
[Title]

- **Explain why you are requesting more information.**

- **Explain the terms you are seeking if any.**

Path on CD-ROM: Management→Goodwill→Charity→Charity—example 7

Gratitude—commendations to presiding chairman or official

[DATE]

[Name/Title]
[Business/Organization Name]
[Address]
[City, State ZIP]

Dear [   ]:

The annual meeting at [Desert Wells] came off without a hitch, [*first name*], and that is a tribute to the staff and officials who worked so hard to put it together. It is also due to your leadership, moderating influence, and hosting abilities demonstrated during [the three-day event]. I don't think I have ever been kept so closely to a clock and schedule. Thanks for your "timely" influence.

As you know, I have worked for numerous chairmen supervising a multitude of directors. Some were better than others, but few measured up to you in ability and influence. I have appreciated your hard work and mentoring over the past two years, [*first name*], and will be truly sorry when your term comes to an end. The organization has grown and prospered significantly under your influence, and so have I.

Kindest regards,

[Name]
[Title]

- **Explain exactly why you're offering your gratitude.**

- **Express regret if person's term is ending.**

Path on CD-ROM: Management→Gratitude→Employee→Employee—example 4

Gratitude—thanking employees

MEMORANDUM

TO: [Marketing]
FROM: [President]
DATE: [   ]
SUBJECT: [Your Recent Assistance]

As you know, [*first name*], I am most impressed by staff people who not only can get things done, but also are not afraid to pitch in for others when the need arises. That is all part of [National Demographics'] teamwork approach, and I was pleased to see that you were not afraid to do your part.

No, strike that. Clearly, you and [*name*] did much more than your parts, particularly when [*name*] was taken ill. I am used to being one of the last ones out the door at night, and it was a pleasant surprise to see the marketing team hard at work, tackling tasks that were not officially even theirs to do.

I plan to report the results of this past quarter at Friday's staff meeting, but I wanted you and [*name*] to know first that we not only did not lose any ground while [*name*] was out, but actually picked up sixteen new accounts. That is due entirely to the hard work of the two of you.

Good show!

- **Explain exactly why you are offering your praise.**

- **Explain what further steps you plan on taking if appropriate.**

Path on CD-ROM: Management→Gratitude→Thanking employees→Thanking employees—example 1

Inquiry—brochure

[DATE]

[Name]
[Company]
[Address]
[City, State ZIP]

Dear [   ]:

[IBEX Industries] is hosting the [national meeting of plant safety officers at the Gold Coast Hotel on October 5, 6 and 7]. We are expecting [1500] attendees.

Would you please ship [1500] of your workshop brochures to me at the address stated above? They need to arrive by [September 15] in order for us to include them in the attendees' welcome packets.

Thank you for your prompt attention to this matter.

Sincerely,

[Name]
[Title]

- Letter specifies number and kind of brochure needed.

- Letter specifies a deadline.

Path on CD-ROM: Management→Inquiry→Brochure→Brochure—example 1

[DATE]

[Name]
[Company]
[Address]
[City, State ZIP]

Dear [   ]:

[Blue Gorge Organic Foods sells organic produce] to the consumer. Over the years, we have used many types of bags to hold the customers' groceries. Because our customers are environmentally aware, we are interested in finding a bag that is both Earth-friendly and strong enough to hold the produce.

Recently, we came across a sample of your plastic bag [(Model #6A)] that seemed to fit the needs of our customers. The sample was both strong and environmentally safe. In order to determine its suitability for our use, would you please send us information on the product and any additional samples you feel would fit our needs?

Thank you in advance for your prompt response.

Sincerely,

[Name]
[Title]

- **Letter describes the customer's needs.**

- **Letter requests more information and a sample.**

Path on CD-ROM: Management→Inquiry→Information→Information—example 1

Invitation—accept

[DATE]

[Name]
[Company]
[Address]
[City, State ZIP]

Dear [   ]:

After reviewing the literature on the [electric forklift] you recently sent, I appreciate the offer to take a firsthand look at your product. Our firm is interested in switching our [propane forklifts to electric ones] and I would like to see how your product compares with what we are currently using.

Thank you for the invitation. I look forward to meeting you at the [Seattle Convention Center on August 5].

Sincerely,

[Name]
[Title]

- **Letter acknowledges the initial invitation.**

- **Letter gives recipient information about the customer's needs and potential interest in the recipient's product.**

Path on CD-ROM: Management→Invitation→Accept→Accept—example 1

Invitation—decline

[DATE]

[Name]
[Company]
[Address]
[City, State ZIP]

Dear [   ]:

I appreciate you sending me your latest [flower and vegetable seed] catalog and the invitation to the sales presentation at the [Regal Hotel on November 21]. However, our company supplies [grass seed solely to the turf and sod industry and your flower and vegetable seeds] do not fit our current line of products.

If we do decide to broaden our merchandise mix, we will contact you. Thank you for thinking of [Green Lawn Company] and we wish you much success with your [seeds].

Sincerely,

[Name]
[Title]

- Letter acknowledges invitation.

- Letter explains why invitation is declined.

Path on CD-ROM: Management→Invitation→Decline→Decline—example 1

Marketing—complaint to opponent

[DATE]

[Name/Title]
[Business/Organization Name]
[Address]
[City, State ZIP]

Dear [   ]:

My campaign manager and I saw your comments about the upcoming election in the leading industry trade journal and wonder what "dirt" you think you might have that you think would cause me to pull out of this election in the 11th hour?

Preliminary polls already are in, and it looks like you are favored to win. But my constituency has yet to be counted, and I would appreciate it if you would keep your fabricated stories about moral turpitude to yourself. You have no proof, and even if you manufacture someone who claims to have been my paramour, my background will do as much to refute that as anything else.

It appears that some politicians do not mind being cast in that light, but, frankly, I do not like it. So please stop it, unless you are ready to prove your contention in a court of law.

Sincere regards,

[Name]
[Title]

- **Identify which specific act offends you.**

- **Explain what steps you are willing to take if the issue is not resolved to your satisfaction.**

Path on CD-ROM: Management→Marketing→Competition→Competition—example 1

Meetings, external—apologizing for a missed external meeting

[DATE]

[Name]
[Company]
[Address]
[City, State ZIP]

Dear [   ]:

Please accept my sincere apology for missing our meeting on [May 7]. I'm terribly sorry that the effects of too full a schedule caused me to overlook the note of our meeting on my calendar. I was looking forward to talking with you.

To make it up to you, I'd like to take you to lunch next week. Would either [Tuesday or Thursday at Mario's Restaurant] work for you? If you can make it, let's discuss our new venture and enjoy some good Italian food.

Thanks for your understanding. Look forward to hearing from you.

Sincerely,

[Name]
[Title]

- **Apologize!**

- **Offer a way to make it up to the person.**

Path on CD-ROM: Management→Meetings-external→Apologizing for missed external meeting→Apologizing for missed external meeting—example 1

Meetings, external—canceling an external meeting

[DATE]

[Name]
[Company]
[Address]
[City, State ZIP]

Dear [   ]:

Thanks for all your hard work on our joint sales venture.

As you know, [JS Manufacturers no longer makes the ABC bolt that was to be the subject of our July 17 meeting]. Because of the change, I'd like to cancel this meeting. If you're interested, I'd like to schedule a meeting about other possible additions to our product line in the next two months.

Sorry for any inconvenience this may have caused. Please let me know if you have any questions. I'll be in touch about the possibility of scheduling another time to get together.

Thank you.

Sincerely,

[Name]
[Title]

- **Explain why the meeting is being canceled.**

- **If appropriate, say you'll be in touch about other times and/or reasons to meet.**

Path on CD-ROM: Management→Meetings-external→Canceling external meeting→Canceling external meeting—example 1

Meetings, internal—annual meeting

MEMORANDUM

TO: [All Stockholders, Directors, and Staff]
FROM: [President's Office]
DATE: [   ]
SUBJECT: [Annual Meeting]

[The Eclipse Corporation's] annual meeting and financial report will be held [Friday, June 9, 1995 in the Festival Ballroom of the Hilton Hotel and Towers, Oklahoma City, Oklahoma, at 10 a.m.] All stockholders, directors, staff, and interested parties are invited to attend.

The [firm's financial condition] will top the agenda, with a comprehensive report by [Chief Financial Officer Marilyn Sobczyk]. The accounting firm of [Shaker, Peabody & Goode, Eclipse Corporation's independent auditing firm], also will present its analysis.

The company's human resources and marketing departments will offer brief insights into the challenges and opportunities facing their specific departments. The meeting will also include a presentation by the president and the election of new board members.

If you cannot attend, please plan to send a proxy for voting purposes. If authorized, a proxy will be appointed on your behalf from among the existing directors.

- **Indicate date, time, and location.**

- **Summarize the events to take place.**

Path on CD-ROM: Management→Meetings-internal→Annual meetings→Annual meetings—example 1

Meetings, internal—canceling an internal meeting via e-mail

TO: [sue@company.com, liz@company.com, peter@company.com]
FROM: [albert@company.com]
RE: [Web team meeting reminder]
CC: [steve@company.com]

Hello Web team.

[Fred] believes that it's the wrong time to pursue electronic payment for the Web site. Because he's the CFO and I take his advice seriously, I am canceling our [1 p.m. meeting on May 15], which was to focus on this topic. We will have another Web team meeting to address other topics soon.

- **Explain the reason for canceling.**

- **Explain what the next step might be.**

Path on CD-ROM: Management→Meetings-internal→Canceling internal meeting email→Canceling internal meeting email—example 1

Meetings, internal—declining an internal meeting

TO: [ ]
FROM: [ ]
SUBJECT: [ ]

[Sue],

I'm sorry I won't be able to make the [marketing team] meeting at [2 p.m. Tuesday]. I will be out of the office at a [conference from Monday through Thursday next week].

If you are circulating the agenda in advance, I would be glad to pass along any ideas I have beforehand. Also, I'd be much obliged if you'd fill me in on what happened at the meeting when I return [from Denver].

If you need anything else for the meeting, please let me know before [Friday].

- **Specify which meeting you will not be attending.**

- **Offer to provide information beforehand, and to follow up on the events of the meeting when you return.**

Path on CD-ROM: Management→Meetings→Declining internal meeting→Declining internal meeting—example 1

Notifying employees of new procedures

INTEROFFICE MEMO

TO: [   ]
FROM: [   ]
DATE: [   ]
SUBJECT: [New procedure for handling computer problems]

The [Information Systems Quality Team] recently developed a new procedure for handling computer problems. [Beginning Monday, July 6] any employee who experiences hardware or software problems with their computer should dial [ext. 808], the number of the new [IS] Help Desk.

The Help Desk will route calls as they come in to available [IS] members. When calling, please state the problem, the type of computer, and the urgency of the call. [IS] members will respond to calls in the order in which they came in and the urgency of the call. Please do not call [IS] members directly. The Help Desk is designed to improve service to the department's internal customers as well as streamline the workload of the department members.

- **Notify employees of new procedure and date effective.**

- **Explain reasoning behind new procedure.**

Path on CD-ROM: Management→Miscellaneous→Notifying employees of new procedures→Notifying employees of new procedures—example 3

Offers to purchase—cover for counter offer

[DATE]

[Name]
[Company]
[Address]
[City, State ZIP]

Dear [   ]:

Thank you for your offer to purchase my [ice cream shop] franchise.

Since you submitted your offer, I have received another proposal from a buyer interested in taking over the business immediately. Unless you can reconsider your May 1 transaction date, I plan to accept this new offer.

Since you submitted your offer first, I want to give you an opportunity to revise it.

If I do not hear from you by [date], I will accept the other offer.

Sincerely,

[Name]
[Title]

- **Explain any new developments fully.**

- **Specify your time frame.**

Path on CD-ROM: Management→Offers to purchase→Cover for counter offer→Cover for counter offer—example 6

Offers to purchase—positive response to query

[DATE]

[Name]
[Company]
[Address]
[City, State ZIP]

Dear [   ]:

I appreciate your query about purchasing our [commuter airline].

Although I am sure that our board of directors will be interested in this sale, I will not have the opportunity to discuss it with them until the beginning of next month. Please submit your formal offer soon, to ensure that I can share it with all board members before their meeting.

On behalf of the board, thank you for your interest. We look forward to receiving your detailed offer by the 28th.

Sincerely,

[Name]
[Title]

- **Do not respond to the offer of a personal consulting assignment; the priority is the desire of the board.**

- **Explain your scheduling parameters.**

Path on CD-ROM: Management→Offers to purchase→Positive response to query re sales status→Positive response to query re sales status—example 3

[DATE]

[Name]
[Company]
[Address]
[City, State ZIP]

Dear [   ]:

Our executives, sales, and marketing staff have been using one type of credit card for the past [11 years]. Since this card company recently increased its rates, we are considering switching our account.

Please send detailed information on annual fees, the interest rate and how it is calculated. Please also include the date and amount of your last increase in annual fees and interest rates.

We also have contacted one additional card company and have invited our current card company to reconsider its fees to us. We plan to make a decision on this issue by the middle of next month.

Sincerely,

[Name]
[Title]

- **Mention why you have decided to explore other vendors.**

- **Include a deadline to spur the reader to action.**

Path on CD-ROM: Management→Operations→Making inquiries-notifications→Making inquiries-notifications—example 16

Operations—making inquiries, example #2

[DATE]

[Name]
[Company]
[Address]
[City, State ZIP]

Dear [   ]:

Yesterday [name], [head of the Downtown Redevelopment Foundation], mentioned that your property at [address] may soon be available for lease.

[I have been searching for a site on which to open an art gallery, studio, and academy, where I will offer classes by area artists in drawing, painting, fiber, and sculpture. I easily can envision how your historic building might be adapted for this purpose and how my business might enhance our downtown.]

Please let me know if and when your building will be available for lease and the terms you are seeking.

[I understand that if I open my business there, the Foundation may help with exterior signage and refurbishing the interior.]

Thank you.

Sincerely,

[Name]
[Title]

- **Share your dream. Enlist the reader's help in fulfilling it.**

- **Mention any extra selling points, such as Foundation support for some improvements.**

Path on CD-ROM: Management→Operations→Making inquiries-notifications→Making inquiries-notifications—example 25

Performance—accepting a promotion

[DATE]

[Name]
[Title]
[Company]
[Address]
[City, State ZIP]

Dear [   ]:

Thank you for your confidence in my abilities. I'm very pleased and honored to accept the promotion to [store manager at our Beaver Valley location]. As we discussed, I'll plan to start work there on [May 2].

I'm looking forward to working hard and making a difference in my new position. Thanks again for the opportunity.

Sincerely,

[Name]
[Title]

- Say thanks for the opportunity to move up.

- Confirm the position and start date.

Path on CD-ROM: Management→Performance→Accepting promotion→Accepting promotion—example 1

Performance—asking an employee to better control expenses

INTEROFFICE MEMORANDUM

TO: [   ]
FROM: [   ]
DATE: [   ]
SUBJECT: [Getting reimbursed for expenses]

We here at [Custom Frame Supplies] like to provide employees with as much latitude as possible. At the same time, a business could not function without a certain number of appropriate guidelines.

For example, only expenses clearly related to business may be reimbursed. Most entertainment expenses are not appropriate for reimbursement. If you feel a particular outing or meal has true business merit, please clear it with me before assuming the company will reimburse you for it. A simple memo—or phone call when the need is immediate—will do the trick.

In addition, individual expenses of more than [$200] always require prior approval, regardless of the category of the expense. Again a simple memo or phone call will be enough to secure approval of a particular expense.

I know you want to avoid not being reimbursed for something that doesn't qualify as a business expense. That's why I'm providing you with the details of these guidelines. If you have any questions, please let me know.

- Explain that you are trying to help the employee by providing these guidelines.

- Explain the details of the guidelines.

Path on CD-ROM: Management→Performance→Asking employee to control expenses→Asking employee to control expenses—example 1

Permissions—authorizing absence after the fact

INTEROFFICE MEMORANDUM

TO: [   ]
FROM: [   ]
DATE: [   ]
SUBJECT: Absence of [date] authorized

On [date], a windstorm struck [suburb] where [name] resides. Due to downed electrical wires, a neighborhood power outage, and trees blocking area roads, he was not able to drive to the office or call in until late in the day. This is to authorize his absence, as indicated in our company policy book, page [7].

- **Briefly explain pertinent details.**

- **Note that the employee was unable to telephone his employer.**

Path on CD-ROM: Management→Permissions→Authorizing absence after the fact→Authorizing absence after the fact—example 3

Permissions—authorizing absence in advance

INTEROFFICE MEMORANDUM

TO: [   ]
FROM: [   ]
DATE: [   ]
SUBJECT: [   ]

This is to authorize a one-day absence for [Kathy Thomas next Thursday, March 17, to attend her father's wedding]. Although [Kathy] is still in her probationary period at [COMPANY], we agreed to her request to attend [this family event] at the time of her hire.

- Many organizational memos are 100 words or less in length.

- Keeping promises to employees builds trust.

Path on CD-ROM: Management→Permissions→Authorizing absence in advance→Authorizing absence in advance—example 1

Permissions—bending company policies

INTEROFFICE MEMORANDUM

TO: [All Employees]
FROM: [   ]
DATE: [   ]
SUBJECT: [Casual day]

[Date] is Casual Dress Day, the one day all year when [company] puts aside business attire in favor of slacks, pullovers, and, yes, even jeans.

On Casual Day, [company] makes a contribution to [city] [Community Foundation]. Any employee who also wishes to donate will receive a [free T-shirt to wear on Casual Day]; however, you do not have to make a donation in order to wear casual clothes on this date.

To sign up or for more information about Casual Day, see [name] at extension [3334].

- **Announce the reason for the relaxing of company policy.**

- **End by explaining how to take action or learn more.**

Path on CD-ROM: Management→Permissions→Bending company policies→Bending company policies—example 8

Permissions—denying a special project

INTEROFFICE MEMORANDUM

TO: [   ]
FROM: [   ]
DATE: [   ]
SUBJECT: [Former employee survey]

You recently requested approval to conduct a mail survey of former employees, as an effort to address our staff turnover problem. I am concerned that a number of former employees will have moved and be difficult to trace, and that this effort may become extremely time-consuming. As a result, I have decided not to approve the survey.

Please consider possible alternatives. For example, you may want to analyze the exit interviews of all employees leaving in the past two years or conduct a survey of current employees to gauge any areas of dissatisfaction.

Let me know what you decide to do.

- Suggest alternative problem-solving techniques.

- Keep the lines of communication open.

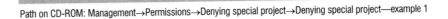

Path on CD-ROM: Management→Permissions→Denying special project→Denying special project—example 1

INTEROFFICE MEMORANDUM

TO: [   ]
FROM: [   ]
DATE: [   ]
SUBJECT: [Farewell lunch]

Yesterday I received your notice about the farewell lunch in the cafeteria, planned for [name], who is leaving [company] for an extended visit to New Zealand. While we all are excited about her upcoming adventure and want to wish her well on the journey, I have decided to decline your request to serve champagne at this luncheon. I agree with the company policy of prohibiting alcohol from the premises, particularly during the middle of the work day.

I plan to attend this lunch and will bring several bottles of sparkling grape juice. I am looking forward to sending off [name] in a style that ensures she will not forget us when she is trekking about the other side of the globe.

- **Clearly state your decision.**

- **Explain that you still intend to support the event itself.**

Policies—informing

M E M O R A N D U M

TO: [All Personnel]
FROM: [Executive Office]
DATE: [   ]
SUBJECT: [No Smoking Policy]

In the interest of good health for all employees, [Westcot Industries] has enacted a formal No Smoking Policy for its executive offices, production facilities, and branch offices around the country. This policy takes effect at midnight May 31.

Health care specialists have proved beyond doubt that smoking is harmful to the general health of both the smoker and those working around him or her. In the interest of the well-being of all employees, no smoking will be permitted on company property before, during, or after formal work hours. This policy extends to management, staff, visitors, suppliers, and family.

In addition, [Westcot Industries] has enacted a policy of reimbursing employees for the costs of all recognized smoking cessation classes or workshops for themselves and their immediate families. Our purpose is not to penalize employees who smoke, but to help them develop a more healthful lifestyle.

Any questions about this or any other company policy should be referred to the executive offices.

- **Avoid personal threats or accusations. Use a neutral tone.**

- **Use actual events or dates to start off the letter or to support your concern.**

Path on CD-ROM: Management→Policies→Informing→Informing—example 1

Policies—punishing employees

INTEROFFICE MEMORANDUM

TO: [Name]
FROM: [   ]
DATE: [   ]
SUBJECT: [Discrimination]

[Your recent memo about progress on filling the open position in your department describes the top three candidates for the job. In building your case for one candidate, you state of another: "In my experience blacks don't work as hard as whites."]

The comment is intolerable and violates our anti-discrimination policy (see page [15] of our personnel handbook).

This citation will be placed in your personnel file. Another comment in the same vein will result in a suspension.

To ensure that [company] makes the best possible hire, report to me by tomorrow precisely how you will compare the professional qualifications of the top three candidates. In addition, please share with me their cover letters, resumes, and portfolios, as well as the notes made by the members of the interview team.

- **Point out the unacceptable behavior.**

- **Take steps to ensure it does not continue.**

Policies—reminding employees

INTEROFFICE MEMORANDUM

TO: [   ]
FROM: [   ]
DATE: [   ]
SUBJECT: [Travel reimbursement]

While reviewing the number of trips we all have taken to conferences and sales meetings this month, I realized that some employees may not be recording and turning in all of their expenses. Following [COMPANY] policy regarding business travel will help everyone's personal bottom line and help us track actual expenses related to each of our product lines.

Please keep accurate records of your mileage and tolls, as well as all receipts for parking and any repair expenses you incur while traveling for [COMPANY].

In addition, please turn in your expense reports and receipts to the business office twice a month, to ensure that you are properly reimbursed for any expenditures you make while on the road.

Thank you for your help in maintaining accurate expense records.

- **Tone is one of concern for proper reimbursement to employees.**

- **Final paragraph assumes employee cooperation.**

Path on CD-ROM: Management→Policies→Reminding employees→Reminding employees—example 4

Problems—asking for assistance

INTEROFFICE MEMORANDUM

TO: [Peer]
FROM: [Name]
DATE: [   ]
SUBJECT: [   ]

I have encountered a difficult situation relating to our business office and hope that you can shed some light on the problem and suggest how to deal with it. [I turned in our department's monthly financial report two days before it was due. Today, a week after the due date, the business manager called to ask why he had not yet received my report. I sent him another copy, which he date-stamped with today's date. He also complained to my supervisor about the late document.]

Today was not the first time this has happened, and there have been other incidents—[like misplacing the travel vouchers submitted by my subordinates, miscalculating their mileage reimbursements, and even arguing about the amount of petty cash I used to buy donuts for a meeting with clients.]

Have you experienced similar problems? How can I improve my relationship with the business office?

I really would appreciate your perspective on this situation.

- Since they share a similar vantage point, peers often can help build relationships in the organization.

- Memo does not belabor a long list of complaints but moves quickly to the key questions.

Path on CD-ROM: Management→Problems→Asking for assistance-peer→Asking for assistance-peer—example 1

Problems—expressing concern over absenteeism

INTEROFFICE MEMORANDUM

TO: [   ]
FROM: [   ]
DATE: [   ]
SUBJECT: [   ]

During your absence yesterday, I was concerned when you did not telephone to let me know why you were not at your desk. As you know, company policy requires us to notify the office when we are out due to illness or other factors.

Notifying the department also enables us to make contingency plans and rework schedules. If you had phoned yesterday morning to let me know that you would be out all day, I could have asked someone to reschedule your appointments and would have assigned the [Foster project] to another staff member.

Please help our department run smoothly by notifying me of all your absences—planned and unplanned.

- **Memo reminds employee of company policy.**

- **Close requests notification of future absences.**

Problems—refusing leave of absence

INTEROFFICE MEMORANDUM

TO: [   ]
FROM: [NAME]
DATE: [   ]
FROM: [   ]

Thank you for the update on [Jenny's] condition. I was glad to learn that she will fully recover so soon. Given her improved condition, I must refuse your request for a [six-week] family leave of absence just as our busiest sales season arrives.

I noted in your personnel file that you have accumulated [15] days of personal leave. Another option would be for you to use these days as needed during the next few weeks. Please let me know if you would like to use this time off, so that I can rearrange our work schedules.

Please also continue to let us know how [Jenny] is progressing.

- **Despite the refusal, memo demonstrates concern for the employee's situation.**

- **Focus at the beginning and end of this memo is on the injured family member.**

Path on CD-ROM: Management→Problems→Refusing to leave of absence-family→Refusing leave of absence-family—example 1

Procedures—change

MEMORANDUM

TO: [Employees of the Midtown Branch]
FROM: [President's Office]
DATE: [   ]
SUBJECT: [Customer Parking]

Those of you who drive to work no doubt have noticed the increasing loss of parking spaces available to customers and staff. What was once our wide-open end-of-the-mall parking lot is now full on a regular basis, thanks to the city's recently enacted Park n Ride program. Those efforts to relieve downtown congestion have increased ours.

It is not likely that the city will change its strategy, especially since the Park n Ride program has become so popular. In fact, we believe that employee and customer parking spaces will continue to decrease over time.

We have had several discussions with mall management, but to no avail. It is time for us to seek our own solutions, but, frankly, we are a little stumped. That is why we are turning to you.

We are looking for suggestions for relieving this parking congestion, and we invite you to submit your best ideas. In addition to helping relieve congestion, the employees whose recommendations are selected will also receive a gift certificate good for dinner for two at [Wally's Beef Palace], along with a day off with pay.

Please submit all suggestions by [September 1]. Thanks for helping us with this thorny issue.

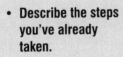

- **Describe the steps you've already taken.**

- **Offer an incentive to encourage participation.**

Path on CD-ROM: Management→Procedures→Change→Change—example 1

Procedures—explaining proper procedures

INTEROFFICE MEMO

TO: [   ]
FROM: [   ]
DATE: [   ]
SUBJECT: Purchasing [Safety Shoes]

[Safety shoes] are required for all employees who [work in areas where a foot injury can occur]. These areas are [list departments]. All employees who are required to [wear safety shoes] are reimbursed for them following [amount of time] of employment.

Here is the procedure for [purchasing the first pair of safety shoes]:

[1. Obtain a shoe authorization form from Human Resources.]

[2. Fill out the form and take it to a designated shoe store.]

[3. Purchase and pay for the shoes.]

[4. Return the receipt to Human Resources.]

[5. After [amount of time] Human Resources will issue a check for the price of the shoes.]

Employees are entitled to [a new pair of safety shoes each year]. [For successive pairs of shoes, follow the above procedure and submit the receipt to Human Resources. The reimbursement check will be issued in the next pay period.]

- **Explain the procedure.**

- **Explain when the employee will be reimbursed for the purchase.**

Path on CD-ROM: Management→Procedures→Explaining proper procedures→Explaining proper procedures—example 5

Recognition—adoption

[DATE]

[Name]
[Address]
[City, State ZIP]

Dear [   ]:

Congratulations on your adoption of [Samuel Jacob]. As new parents, how lucky you must feel to be able to share your love with a special child.

We at [Mountain View Bank] are delighted to share in your joy.

Sincerely,

[Name]
[Title]

- **Letter expresses congratulations.**

- **Because adoption is occasionally a sensitive topic, the letter just refers to the recipients being new parents and doesn't go into detail about how they became parents.**

Path on CD-ROM: Management→Recognition→Adoption→Adoption—example 1

Recognition—anniversary of doing business

[DATE]

[Name/Title]
[Business/Organization Name]
[Address]
[City, State ZIP]

Dear [   ]:

Congratulations on the 10-year anniversary of [*name of company*]. Your service to the city's small businesses is without comparison, and we are pleased that by helping others prosper, you also have made your mark.

Ten years ago, the company was a mere idea of [*name of founder*], who came from a small firm where a little capital, a little consulting, and a lot of hard work can make a big difference. By starting [*name of company*], [*name of founder*] turned that belief into a commitment, and that commitment into a successful business.

Business in [Central City] is prospering, and [*name of company*] has played an important role in making that happen. Again, congratulations on ten years of service, and thank you for your excellent work.

Best regards,

[Name]
[Title]

- **Show your knowledge of the company's background.**

- **Explain why you think the business deserves special praise for their anniversary.**

Path on CD-ROM: Management→Recognition→Anniversary of employment→Anniversary of employment—example 4

Recognition—birth

[DATE]

[Name]
[Address]
[City, State ZIP]

Dear [   ]:

Congratulations on the birth of your baby boy, [Jason]. The birth of a baby gives all of us hope for the future as well as an opportunity for joy and celebration.

We wish you, [Jason and Jennifer], many sleep-filled nights and lots of laughter and good times.

Cordially,

[Name]
[Title]

- Letter extends congratulations.

- Letter ends with an upbeat, positive note.

Path on CD-ROM: Management→Recognition→Birth→Birth—example 1

References—declining to give a reference

[DATE]

[Name]
[Title]
[Company]
[Address]
[City, State ZIP]

Dear [   ]:

It was really a pleasure having you on staff. I remember your commitment and hard work.

My rule about references is to provide them for people I've either worked with for at least two years or known well for at least five. I checked our employment records and found that you worked here from [January 1995 to March 1996]. I regret that the history of our relationship is not long enough for me to feel comfortable providing you a reference at this time.

Perhaps you would be able to get a reference from [John], whom you worked for much longer than for me.

My best to you in your job search.

Sincerely,

[Name]
[Title]

- **If possible, provide a concrete reason why you can't provide the reference.**

- **Offer an idea for someone else the reader could contact, if you know of one.**

Path on CD-ROM: Management→References→Declining to give references→Declining to give references—example 1

References—providing a reference for a terminated employee (competent)

[DATE]

[Name]
[Address]
[City, State ZIP]

Dear [   ]:

It is my pleasure to provide you with a reference for [name].

[name] was employed here as the [position] from [date] to [date]. During that time, [s/he] performed above my expectations in the areas of [area], [area] and [area]. In addition, [s/he] [achievement].

It is true that [company] terminated [name]'s employment here. Please understand that this happened as a result of financial problems and the consolidating of positions, not because of any deficiency in [name]'s performance.

If you have any further questions, please feel free to call me.

Sincerely,

[Name]
[Title]

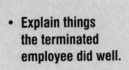

- **Explain things the terminated employee did well.**

- **If the termination was not for bad performance, say so.**

Path on CD-ROM: Management→References→Providing reference for terminated employee-competent→Providing reference for terminated employee-competent—example 1

References—providing a reference for a terminated employee (incompetent)

[DATE]

[Name]
[Address]
[City, State ZIP]

Dear [   ]:

[name] was employed at [company] from [date] to [date] as [position]. [name] was [positive characteristic or ability].

If you have further questions, please contact me.

Sincerely,

[Name]
[Title]

- **Confirm that the person was formerly employed at the company, in what position and when.**

- **Say something positive about the person and leave it at that.**

Path on CD-ROM: Management→References→Providing reference for terminated employee-incompetent→Providing reference for terminated employee-incompetent—example 1

Reminder

[DATE]

[Name]
[Company]
[Address]
[City, State ZIP]

Dear [   ]:

If your calendar is as full as mine is, sometimes meetings and dates just slip by despite my good intentions.

This is just a reminder that the [Computer Users' group] will meet on [Tuesday evening, March 9 for the monthly business meeting]. The meeting will be held at [6:00 p.m. in the Royal Room of the Grace Hotel].

[Please bring the information on disk drives that members were asked to research.]

We hope to see you there.

Sincerely,

[Name]
[Title]

- **Letter reminds recipient of meeting date, time and place.**

- **Letter prompts recipient to remember the assignment from the last meeting.**

Path on CD-ROM: Management→Reminder→Example→Example—example 1

Report to a peer

INTEROFFICE MEMORANDUM

TO: [   ]
FROM: [   ]
DATE: [   ]
SUBJECT: Suggestions for Improving the Company Newsletter

Thanks for requesting my input in improving the [*Inquirer*]. I am delighted to offer my suggestions.

I believe that the newsletter serves a vital purpose in keeping the lines of communication open between management and employees. It also acts as a "good news" vehicle and helps keep the rumor mill quiet. It seems to be meeting those goals quite well.

As far as ideas for improving the publication, I would like to suggest the following:

[•   A new font style and size

The current font style is quite old-fashioned and the 9 pt. type is extremely difficult to read. You might want to check out some easy-to-read fonts like Garamond and Palatino.]

[•   A new layout

The current four-column layout means words are hyphenated in odd places and lots of gaps appear between words. A two-column layout would improve readability.]

[•   Additional photographs

The old adage, "a picture is worth a thousand words," certainly is true. More pictures of employee activities would help the employees feel ownership to the publication.]

[•   Additional features on employees]

[1.   I would like to see more features on employees and less on management. This newsletter should connect the employees at different plants together rather than be a PR vehicle for management.]
[2.   A "Letters to the Editor" column would give readers an opportunity to ask questions and "sound off" on their likes and dislikes.]
[3.   A column on birthdays, anniversaries and other significant life events would make the newsletter more personal.]

I would be happy to discuss any one of these items in greater detail. The [*Inquirer*] has a solid foundation and a great deal of potential. I am all for improving the publication to make it even better.

- **Use an informal tone when the report is about an every day matter.**

- **Be specific and concise. Reports help executives make informed decisions.**

Path on CD-ROM: Management→Report→Report to peer→Report to peer—example 1

Requests—asking for assistance

INTEROFFICE MEMORANDUM

TO: [Name]
FROM: [   ]
DATE: [   ]
SUBJECT: [Trade Expo]

When you attend the Trade Expo next week, please take [1,000] [company] brochures with you.

I have made arrangements with the event organizers to display our brochures on the information table adjacent to the registration desk.

Thank you for your help in publicizing our company's services to the industry.

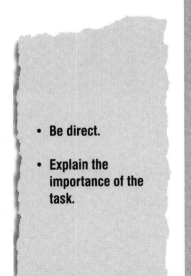

- **Be direct.**

- **Explain the importance of the task.**

Path on CD-ROM: Management→Requests→Asking for assistance-subordinate→Asking for assistance-subordinate—example 11

Requests—denial

[DATE]

[Name/Title]
[Business/Organization Name]
[Address]
[City, State ZIP]

Dear [   ]:

On [May 31], we received your letter requesting an appointment with our client, [Pennsylvania Matchlocks Inc.] After conferring with principals of the firm, we regret to inform you that we must respectfully decline your request.

[Mr. Taylor Prince], president of [Pennsylvania Matchlocks Inc.], has informed us that his firm is no longer interested in doing business with [Hookline & Sinker Inc.] What's more, [Mr. Prince] has retained our office to consider legal proceedings against your firm. To date, no action has been taken, but we are reviewing options.

We will be in touch in the near future concerning the matter of [the missing shipment]. Until then, we will decline all future requests for an appointment.

Sincerely,

[Name]
[Title]

- **Acknowledge receipt of request for an appointment.**

- **Indicate how you will deal with this issue in the future.**

Path on CD-ROM: Management→Requests→Denial→Denial—example 1

Reservations—confirm

[DATE]

[Name]
[Company]
[Address]
[City, State ZIP]

Dear [   ]:

Thank you for choosing the [Mayflower Hotel, Denver's finest business hotel]. This is to confirm the reservation for [Mr. Tony Ruiz] for [three nights, May 30, June 1 and June 2]. [Mr. Ruiz] has requested [a single non-smoking room with a king-size bed]. The charge [for the room] will be [$165 per night].

[The hotel will hold his room until 6 p.m. If Mr. Ruiz expects to arrive late, will he please notify us before May 30?]

We look forward to welcoming [Mr. Ruiz] to [Denver].

Sincerely,

[Name]
[Title]

- **Acknowledge the reservation and specify the dates and the rate.**

- **State the hotel policy on late arrivals.**

Path on CD-ROM: Management→Reservations→Confirm→Confirm—example 3

Response for support

INTEROFFICE MEMORANDUM

TO: [   ]
FROM: [   ]
DATE: [   ]
SUBJECT: [Your support of the Brownfields project]

When I took on the [Brownfields] project, I knew it was a career risk. [Greyson Environmental Engineering] had never done anything like this before. And since the wastewater conversion project was not a huge success, most people would not have chosen that time to propose a new direction. But the opportunity was there and I believed that we needed to act on it quickly.

Because of your support, [Greyson is two weeks away from unveiling a new technology that will dramatically impact the way brownfields are treated]. Preliminary results show that the technology will allow [land that had been contaminated with heavy metals, petroleum and other hazardous wastes to be reclaimed for other uses].

Your support for the project was immeasurable in getting the go-ahead and the financing. Thank you for trusting in it and me.

- **Acknowledge the importance of the support received.**

- **Express gratitude for the support.**

Path on CD-ROM: Management→Miscellaneous→Response for support→Response for support—example 1

Shareholders—accepting a board member's resignation

[DATE]

[Name]
[Company]
[Address]
[City, State ZIP]

Dear [   ]:

I was sorry to receive your letter explaining your recent health problems, as well as your notice of resignation from [company's] board of directors. I will hope for a full recovery.

Thank you for your valuable service on the board, [your promotion of our strategic plan, and your knowledgeable contributions related to the global marketplace]. [Company] certainly would not have progressed so far in the last [two years] without your efforts.

You will continue to receive our company newsletter and, of course, the annual report. I hope you will contact us occasionally to let us know how you are doing.

Best wishes,

[Name]
[Title]

- **Acknowledge the resignation.**

- **List several of the reader's contributions to the board.**

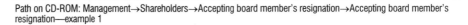

Path on CD-ROM: Management→Shareholders→Accepting board member's resignation→Accepting board member's resignation—example 1

Shareholders—acknowledgement of intention to attend annual meeting

[DATE]

[Name]
[Company]
[Address]
[City, State ZIP]

Dear [   ]:

I was glad to learn that you will be attending the annual meeting of [Mid-States Coal, Inc., set for April 29 at our corporate headquarters, 99999 Wabash Ave. in Chicago].

Enclosed are lunch tickets for you and your spouse, as well as a map to our company headquarters.

I look forward to meeting you on [April 29].

Sincerely,

[Name]
[Title]

- **Brief note acknowledges shareholder's intent to attend the meeting.**

- **Close is congenial, welcoming.**

Path on CD-ROM: Management→Acknowledgement of intention to attend annual meeting→Acknowledgement of intention to attend annual meeting—example 1

Shareholders—congratulations on annual report

[DATE]

[Name]
[Company]
[Address]
[City, State ZIP]

Dear [   ]:

Thank you for sending a copy of your outstanding annual report.

I was especially interested to read about [your exceptional success in providing software to healthcare professionals, following several years of significant investment in this area. Our own company has been providing more and more management seminars in the healthcare arena.]

I would like to discuss with you our mutual interests in serving this sector and will call to set an appointment the next time I visit your city.

In the meantime, congratulations on a fine report and an exceptional year.

Sincerely,

[Name]
[Title]

- **Letter mentions specific information found it the annual report.**

- **Congratulatory note serves as a springboard to possible future collaboration.**

Path on CD-ROM: Management→Shareholders→Congratulations on annual report→Congratulations on annual report—example 1

Transmittal

[DATE]

[Name]
[Organization]
[Address]
[City, State ZIP]

Dear [   ]:

I have enclosed the report on the [customer surveys that we conducted in the greater Philadelphia area].

The [survey results] revealed that [your target customer is female, 35–60, affluent and shops at your store at least once a week. This group should respond well to the multiple on-site events that you plan to schedule.]

Let me take this opportunity to thank [Michael George] of [your staff]. His input was extremely helpful in [designing the questionnaire and his knowledge of the area helped us focus our results].

If you have any questions regarding our findings, please call me at [888-999-7654]. It has been a pleasure assisting your company with its [sales objectives].

Sincerely,

[Name]
[Title]

- **Explain the enclosed document.**

- **Highlight a major point to capture your reader's attention.**

Path on CD-ROM: Management→Transmittal→Documents→Documents—example 5

Public Relations and Publicity

Although sometimes public relations letters are sent to customers or vendors directly, most often they get the attention of the public by first getting the attention of the media. In contrast to sales letters, the goal of public relations letters is to improve or clarify an organization's public image, *not* to increase sales directly.

How can you catch the attention of the public through the media? For starters, consider the things that journalism students learn make a story "newsworthy":

- Audience: will the media outlet's readers be interested?
- Impact: does the news affect many people?
- Prominence: are important people involved?
- Oddity: are you giving them something out of the ordinary?
- Proximity: is the event you are sponsoring happening right in the city or across the state?
- Timeliness: are you asking the media to cover Christmas in February?
- Magnitude: are so many people coming or interested that the story must get covered?
- Conflict: will there be a debate over the issue?

If one or more of these elements is present in your story, the media will be much more likely to cover it. Even if your public relations letters are sent directly to customers, vendors, or potential partners in charity work, make sure they contain "newsworthy" information. It will help get them read.

Accepting a press interview

[DATE]

[Name]
[Company]
[Address]
[City, State ZIP]

Dear [   ]:

Thank you for your interest in writing about the [remodeling industry and A+ Contractors in particular]. Our company president, [Ed Tyler], would be happy to be interviewed for your article.

[Ed] is in the office [Wednesday through Friday of next week]. Would you be available [Wednesday at 2:30 p.m.]? If so, I will have [Ed] call you then. If not, we can arrange another time. Either way, please let me know.

Thanks again for your interest. Please let me know if I can be of any further assistance.

Sincerely,

[Name]
[Title]

- Be friendly.

- Offer a meeting time and other times to meet if available.

Accepting an invitation to serve on a board

[DATE]

[Name]
[Company]
[Address]
[City, State ZIP]

Dear [   ]:

It would be my pleasure to serve on the board of [Afternoon Companions]. I do wholeheartedly support the group's cause. Please let me know the time, date, and place of the first meeting I should attend.

Thank you for your assistance.

Sincerely,

[Name]
[Title]

- **Indicate your acceptance.**

- **Request needed information.**

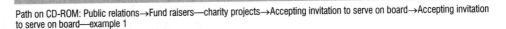

Path on CD-ROM: Public relations→Fund raisers—charity projects→Accepting invitation to serve on board→Accepting invitation to serve on board—example 1

Accompanying a speaker's payment

[DATE]

[Name]
[Address]
[City, State ZIP]

Dear [   ]:

Thank you for speaking at our [event] in [month]. Your session was given very high marks by conference participants. We are so pleased we would be glad to recommend you to the organizers of other conferences.

I'm enclosing your fee in payment for your talk. Thanks again for your good efforts.

Sincerely,

[Name]
[Title]

- **If you really liked the speaker, see if you can offer a bonus of some kind.**

- **State which conference and date for which you are paying.**

Path on CD-ROM: Public relations→Events→Accompanying speaker's payment→Accompanying speaker's payment—example 2

Acknowledging request for a donation

[DATE]

[Name]
[Address]
[City, State ZIP]

Dear [   ]:

Thank you for the materials you sent about [organization] as part of your fund-raising drive. You should be very proud of the good work you are doing in our community.

I wanted to let you know that I have passed your packet along to [our community outreach team], which makes all decisions about corporate giving for [company]. In general, [the team] puts together the year's [outreach] funding budget [once a year in [month], as part of our overall planning and budgeting process].

Although [the team] decides on actions, I am the contact person for correspondence surrounding our contributions. If you send any other materials, I will be glad to forward them on to the team. If it decides to grant you funds, I will let you know.

Thanks again for keeping us informed of your good work.

Sincerely,

[Name]
[Title]

- **Thank the group for sending materials.**

- **Let the contact know what is happening with their request.**

Path on CD-ROM: Public relations→Fund raisers—charity projects→Acknowledging request for donation→Acknowledging request for donation—example 1

Addressing bad news

[DATE]

[Name/Title]
[Business/Organization Name]
[Address]
[City, State ZIP]

Dear [   ]:

We have heard of some wild schemes to raise public funds, [Mayor Stockton], but never before have we heard of a [$50] parking fee for out-of-town commuters. We think the general public will be as resistant to the idea as we are, and we doubt that you will get the support you need to pass the measure.

Consider the facts: Roughly [40] percent of the city's working population lives outside the city limits. In the case of some companies, that number grows to nearly [80 percent] of the workforce. Employers that are unable to ante up for every out-of-towner they have working for them face one more expense in recruiting talent. And enough of these hurdles could send employers looking for cheaper offices in one of the surrounding communities, one that would welcome the business and would not tax commuters.

We urge you to reconsider your plan. It will only drive a bigger wedge between the business community and your office.

Thanks for the consideration. We think this is in the best interests of all.

Regards,

[Name]
[Title]

- **Reference facts that support your case.**

- **Be polite.**

Path on CD-ROM: Public relations→Announcements→Bad news→Bad news—example 1

Advising employees about dealing with the press

INTEROFFICE MEMORANDUM

TO: [   ]
FROM: [   ]
DATE: [   ]
SUBJECT: [Managing media inquiries]

One of these days you're going to answer your office phone and find yourself talking to someone who works for a press organization. This memo will explain [WCCU's] procedure for handling media requests.

It's a part of the job of people with titles including "editor, publisher, reporter, writer, researcher, and reviewer" to talk with expert sources and to include those sources' comments and opinions in their articles.

To help keep track of the information [WCCU] employees give to the press, the company requires that all media inquiries be directed to our media contact, [Irene Scott. Irene] will determine whether the interview should be granted and how it will be conducted.

If you have further questions about handling the media, please see [Irene].

- **Offer specific titles that will help employees distinguish press people.**

- **Use a tone that makes press inquiries seem normal, not scary.**

Path on CD-ROM: Public relations→Employees→Advising employees about dealing with the press→Advising employees about dealing with the press—example 1

Advising staff about discussing competitors

INTEROFFICE MEMORANDUM

TO: [   ]
FROM: [   ]
DATE: [   ]
SUBJECT: [Talking publicly about competitors]

The right to freedom of speech is limited only when that right fringes on the rights of others.

While [MMS] tries to give employees as much latitude as possible, we do ask that you consider carefully any comments you make about our competitors in a public setting. Comments about competitors, whether positive or negative, can be construed by the press or the public as having deeper meaning. These comments can also have a real impact on the public image of [MMS].

Often a good way to handle questions about competitors is to turn it around to focus on [MMS] and its products. [For example, if someone asks, "What do you think of the MDB light bulb?" you could answer, "MMS has a spectacular new soft white bulb that saves on consumers' energy bills."]

If you have any questions about this request, please let me know.

- **Explain what behavior to avoid.**

- **Suggest an alternative behavior.**

Path on CD-ROM: Public relations→Employees→Advising staff about discussing competitors→Advising staff about discussing competitors—example 1

Agreeing to contribute an article

[DATE]

[Name]
[Address]
[City, State ZIP]

Dear [   ]:

Thank you so much for inviting me to contribute an article to the [date] issue of [publication] on the topic of [topic]. It will be my pleasure to prepare it for you.

My understanding of your needs is the following:

Article topic: [topic]

Length: [number of words or another measure]

Deadline: [date]

Need for photos or graphics: [detail, suggest press photo]

Format of article: [submit on disk, as E-mail, text format or other]

If I have misunderstood you on any of these points—or if I have missed something, please let me know. Otherwise, I'll send you the article by [deadline].

Thanks again for this opportunity.

Sincerely,

[Name]
[Title]

- **Thank the editor for the opportunity to contribute.**

- **Ask for a response if any of the expectations detailed are incorrect.**

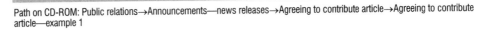

Path on CD-ROM: Public relations→Announcements—news releases→Agreeing to contribute article→Agreeing to contribute article—example 1

Agreeing with an editorial

[DATE]

[Name]
[Company]
[Address]
[City, State ZIP]

Dear [   ]:

The members and staff of [Civic Businesses United] agree wholeheartedly with your assertion that the [west side parking problem needs to be solved—and that building a parking ramp is the proper solution].

[Our customers struggle to come to our places of business, especially during busy lunch hours and commute times. They enjoy coming to the west side, however, because of its historic appearance and lovely gardens.]

[Building a parking ramp in keeping with the area's current architectural style is an excellent way to make it easier for city residents to do business on the west side, while still protecting what makes the neighborhood so special.]

Thank you for your excellent editorial.

Sincerely,

[Name]
[Title]

- **Agree with what's been said already.**

- **Provide details from your particular perspective about the issue.**

Path on CD-ROM: Public relations→Communications→Agreeing with an editorial→Agreeing with an editorial—example 1

Announcing a move to customers

[DATE]

[Name]
[Company]
[Address]
[City, State ZIP]

Dear [   ]:

We're pleased to let you know that [UWV] is successfully serving so many customers that we've outgrown our current business location! Fortunately, we've found another site not too far from the first that will suit our needs nicely.

We'll be moving into our new offices at [2341 Montrose St. during the first week of October]. All of our phone lines will remain the same. We have a plan in place that will help us serve you even while the move is taking place. Still, if there's any hitch that week, we hope you will forgive us.

Soon we'll be writing to invite you to an open house and office warming. We're very excited about our new space. When we are enjoying extra elbow room, we know we'll be able to serve you even better!

Sincerely,

[Name]
[Title]

- Note the location of the new office and any new phone numbers.

- Let customers know what will happen to their orders during the move.

Path on CD-ROM: Public relations→Announcements→Announcing a move to customers→Announcing a move to customers—example 1

Denying permission to use copyrighted material

[DATE]

[Name]
[Title]
[Company]
[Address]
[City, State ZIP]

Dear [   ]:

Thank you for your interest in using [my book] as part of your event. I always like to provide community service whenever possible.

Unfortunately, [my publisher and I agree that the context of this use is in direct opposition to the ideals of the characters in the book.] I regret that we cannot give you permission to read or reprint the book in this context.

Thanks again for your interest.

Sincerely,

[Name]
[Title]

- Show appreciation for the person's interest in using your material.

- Explain how the proposed use would be inappropriate for your material.

Path on CD-ROM: Public relations→Permissions→Denying permission to use copyrighted material→Denying permission to use copyrighted material—example 2

Disagreeing with an editorial

[DATE]

[Name]
[Company]
[Address]
[City, State ZIP]

Dear [   ]:

While we have agreed with many of your previous editorials, we do not concur with your opinion about [how to discourage panhandling. Instead we believe that a gentle approach will work just fine].

[You supported the city council's proposal to write and enforce stiff penalties, including jail time, for people who panhandle on the city's pedestrian mall. This approach seems far too harsh.]

[What if each person and company made it their business to donate food, money, and clothes to help the panhandlers? What if the panhandlers knew where they could go to get it? What if we all volunteered time to staff this center? Surely this is a more humanitarian way to handle the situation.]

[I'll be the first to volunteer monetary and personnel resources.]

Thanks for taking time to understand our position. We encourage you to reconsider yours.

Sincerely,

[Name]
[Title]

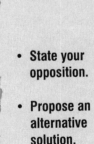

- **State your opposition.**

- **Propose an alternative solution.**

Path on CD-ROM: Public relations→Communications→Disagreeing with an editorial→Disagreeing with an editorial—example 1

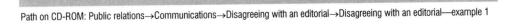

Explaining a reduction in corporate earnings

[DATE]

[Name]
[Company]
[Address]
[City, State ZIP]

Dear Stockholder:

Just like successful people, successful businesses grow and change over time. As people grow up, they sometimes hold different ideas from their parents about how their lives should progress. Ultimately, successful people put their ideas to the test and come out on top.

[UYFR] is in the development stages of a product we expect will have huge earning potential in the next five years. Funding this and other projects is ensuring future prosperity while somewhat reducing corporate earnings in the current quarter.

This kind of slight change is only normal on the path to success. We have the human resources, technology, and vision to reach our highest goals.

Sincerely,

[Name]
[Title]

- **Put the situation in perspective with an analogy if possible.**

- **Focus on future earning potential.**

Path on CD-ROM: Public relations→Explanations→Explaining a reduction in corporate earnings→Explaining a reduction in corporate earnings—example 1

Getting permission to use someone else's material

[DATE]

[Name]
[Title]
[Company]
[Address]
[City, State ZIP]

Dear [   ]:

What a great speech! I always enjoy your talks at the [Rotary Club].

[As you know, I'm working on a book about great opening lines for talks and presentations. Would it be all right with you if I used your ice breaker from last week's Rotary Club talk? Of course, I would give you credit for developing it, and I'd provide you with a copy of the book when it's published.] Plus, it could be some great publicity for your speaking tour.

You're a superb speaker and I hope you'll be comfortable with me including this piece of your presentation in my book. Please give me a call at your convenience.

Thanks for considering this.

Sincerely,

[Name]
[Title]

- If you know the speaker, make the request as personalized as possible.

- Use compliments carefully to encourage a positive response.

Path on CD-ROM: Public relations→Permissions→Getting permission to use someone else's material→Getting permission to use someone else's material—example 1

Letter asking to make a speech

[DATE]

[Name]
[Company]
[Address]
[City, State ZIP]

Dear [   ]:

[Dolls: Breaking Them Out.] This is the title of the talk I'd like to present at your upcoming ["Dolls on the Horizon"] conference.

This talk could cover [how to introduce children to dolls, including how to choose the right doll for a particular child]. The program can be tailored to the time you allot for conference sessions.

[As the owner of a doll shop and publisher of a dollhouse magazine, I can offer many personal stories of children and dolls as well as extensive experience from reading industry research in the talk.] In addition, I have experience speaking at several other [doll] conferences.

Please let me know if you have any questions or require additional information about my proposed speech. Thank you for considering me.

Sincerely,

[Name]
[Title]

- **Give the talk a catchy name.**

- **Provide enough of your background to show why you're a good candidate for giving this speech.**

Path on CD-ROM: Public relations→Requests→Letter asking to make a speech→Letter asking to make a speech—example 1

Requesting referrals for donations

[DATE]

[Name/Title]
[Business/Organization Name]
[Address]
[City, State ZIP]

Dear [   ]:

Thank you for your generous contribution to the [Ulysses S. Grant Elementary School Scholarship Fund]. We have already put your funds to work on [the children's behalf, and the new semester in their educational laboratory already has begun].

We see a need to expand the program in order to address [many of the students' home needs]. We are seeking additional donations from previous contributors, or referrals to like-minded individuals who both understand and appreciate what it is that [Balfour University] seeks to accomplish. If you cannot contribute again so soon, would you please complete the attached card with the names and addresses of friends and relatives who you think might appreciate and support our efforts.

As in the past, we appreciate your continued support. Help us help the next generation gain better control of its own destiny.

Sincerely,

[Name]
[Title]

- **Thank the contributor.**

- **Explain what you're requesting the money for.**

Path on CD-ROM: Public relations→Community→Donation→Donation—example 5

Responding to a solicitation positively

[DATE]

[Name/Title]
[Business/Organization Name]
[Address]
[City, State ZIP]

Dear [   ]:

Other than those associated with classroom survival, few educators take chances anymore. I applaud what [Balfour's School of Education] is attempting to do and am happy to enclose my contribution to your efforts.

Please keep me informed of your activities. If [Balfour] can pull off such a program in its community, there is no telling what is possible for schools across the country.

Good luck,

[Name]
[Title]

- **Note that your contribution is enclosed.**

- **Ask to be kept up to date.**

Path on CD-ROM: Public relations→Community→Donation→Donation—example 4

Saying thanks for positive coverage

[DATE]

[Name]
[Company]
[Address]
[City, State ZIP]

Dear [   ]:

Accurate reporting is a practiced skill; writing well is an innate art. You seem to have the knack for both.

Thank you so much for doing such an excellent job on your recent article that included [TBC Jewelers]. You got all the facts right and wove them together into a most readable story. Good work!

If I can ever be of help for a future article, please don't hesitate to call me. Thanks again.

Sincerely,

[Name]
[Title]

- **Note your appreciation of the accuracy of the article.**

- **Offer to provide information for future articles.**

Path on CD-ROM: Public relations→Thank you→Saying thanks for positive coverage→Saying thanks for positive coverage—example 1

Thanking for funds received

[DATE]

[Name]
[Company]
[Address]
[City, State ZIP]

Dear [   ]:

Thank you for your contribution of [$75] to the [Cassonville volunteer fire department]. You are helping to make a difference here in [Cassonville].

[Please keep the fire department in mind throughout the year as you consider ways to improve the well being of your family and your community. Some donors find it convenient to make a monthly commitment of $15 or more to ensure the good work of the volunteers is supported, even after the end of the annual fundraising campaign.]

[If you'd ever like a tour of the fire department, we'd be happy to show it to you.] Again, thank you for your support.

Sincerely,

[Name]
[Title]

- **Say thanks for the actual amount contributed if possible.**

- **Suggest other, additional contributions.**

Path on CD-ROM: Public relations→Thank you→Thanking for funds received→Thanking for funds received—example 1

Customer Service

When writing customer service letters, a direct approach is best. The majority of customer service letters either to a customer or from a customer involve the exchange of information. The letters either ask for or give specific facts so that the company can satisfy the customer.

Keys to successful customer service letters include:

- Be specific.
- Watch the tone of the letter. Even if the customer is wrong, how you present that information can directly impact on whether that customer stays or leaves.
- Ask for what information you need to help the customer.
- Use a positive or negative buffer when delivering negative news.
- Restate the information to ensure you have it right.
- Specify dates, prices, order numbers, invoice numbers and any other data that will help you serve the customer.
- Draw the customer's attention to a new product or service or sell the customer on your company.
- Always thank the customer for his/her business.
- Always encourage future business.

Complaints

When responding to complaints from customers, remember that the customer may not always be right, but he/she is the customer. A key element in responding to complaints is to treat that person as you would want to be treated. It is easier to keep a customer than to replace them. Letters responding to complaints from customers should:

- Acknowledge the complaint and reference how you heard about it.
- Promise to check on the complaint.
- Tell the customer how and when you will respond to the complaint and then do it.
- Explain the situation that caused the complaint.
- Explain how the situation that caused the complaint was fixed, if appropriate.
- Apologize for the inconvenience caused by the situation.
- If your company did not cause the situation, tell the customer that.
- Help the customer resolve the situation if appropriate.
- Thank the customer for his/her business.
- Thank the customer for his/her understanding of the situation.
- Encourage future business.

Acknowledging complaint example #1

[DATE]

[Name]
[Address]
[City, State ZIP]

Dear [   ]:

Your letter of [June 2] caused me to review the ad we placed in the [*Journal-Sentinel* newspaper last Sunday]. In reviewing the copy I can understand how you would interpret the [50% off headline as implying that everything in the store was 50% off].

I apologize for this misunderstanding. I have sent a copy of your letter and the ad to our advertising department and asked them to be diligent when approving copy for publication.

I hope you continue to shop with us as we truly wish to keep serving your new fashion needs.

Sincerely,

[Name]
[Title]

- **Acknowledge the complaint and explain how the complaint was handled.**

- **Apologize for the error, if necessary.**

Path on CD-ROM: Customer service→Complaints→Acknowledging→Acknowledging—example 1

Acknowledging complaint example #2

[DATE]

[Name]
[Address]
[City, State ZIP]

Dear [   ]:

I'm sorry your last visit to [Toothful Dental] was a stressful one. The noise you referenced in your letter of [November 21st] was caused by a remodeling project that will be completed next week.

I know the noise from the extra workers and the remodeling equipment adds a lot of confusion to a place that's usually more subdued.

I regret that the noise distressed you and made your visit unpleasant. I trust your next visit will be much quieter.

Sincerely,

[Name]
[Title]

- **Acknowledge the customer's correspondence.**

- **Explain the situation that caused the customer's complaint.**

Path on CD-ROM: Customer service→Complaints→Acknowledging→Acknowledging—example 2

COMPLAINTS

Acknowledging purchase has been shipped

[DATE]

[Name/Title]
[Business/Organization Name]
[Address]
[City, State ZIP]

Dear [   ]:

Thank you for your letter of [*date*] regarding your order for [*name and quantity of product*]. Our internal research has uncovered a bottleneck in our fulfillment procedures that has delayed several shipments, including yours. The error has been rectified and will not occur again. Your order has now been processed and shipped.

Please accept our apologies for the delay. If any more problems occur with either this or other orders, please contact me, and I will personally take care of the matter.

Sincerely,

[Name]
[Title]

- **Acknowledge receiving the customer's letter.**

- **Indicate how the problem has been resolved, and apologize.**

Path on CD-ROM: Customer service→Complaints from customer→Acknowledging→Acknowledging—example 1

Adjustments

[DATE]

[Name]
[Company]
[Address]
[City, State ZIP]

Dear [   ]:

Please accept our sincere apologies for the [rude behavior] you experienced [while shopping at our store]. [La Petite Boutique] prides itself on providing superb customer service and this incident is simply unacceptable.

We have spoken with the individual responsible for the behavior and [she] is no longer with the store. We have also enclosed a [discount coupon good for 50% off of any item under $100]. We hope these actions begin to ease the embarrassment you felt.

Thank you for bringing this matter to our attention. We hope to see you at our [end-of-season clearance] sale, which begins next week.

Sincerely,

[Name]
[Title]

- **Acknowledge the problem and apologize for the incident.**

- **Offer a satisfactory solution and encourage future business.**

Path on CD-ROM: Customer service→Complaints from customer→Adjustments→Adjustments—example 7

COMPLAINTS

Defending company

[DATE]

[Name]
[Address]
[City, State ZIP]

Dear [   ]:

Thank you for informing us about your experience with our [item 1]. [Company] prides itself on the quality and dependability of our [products] and always welcomes feedback from our customers.

I can appreciate your disappointment over the failure of our [item 1]. However, we cannot [replace your item because we no longer manufacture it. In fact, that item has not been made for [amount of time]].

[We replaced the [item] with [item 2], which is available at many major home stores. The store closest to you is [list store].]

Sincerely,

[Name]
[Title]

- **Acknowledge the customer's request.**

- **Explain why you cannot or will not honor it.**

Path on CD-ROM: Customer service→Complaints from customer→Defending company→Defending company—example 1

COMPLAINTS

Explaining—as a customer

[DATE]

[Name/Title]
[Business/Organization Name]
[Address]
[City, State ZIP]

Dear [   ]:

For the last [*number*] years, we have enjoyed dealing with your firm. The quality of merchandise has been high, and the service courteous and prompt. Frankly, we have had no complaints. Until now.

[*Outline nature and detail of complaint.*]

We would appreciate a swift resolution of this matter. To date we have enjoyed our ongoing working relationship. If this situation is not rectified, however, that relationship may have to end.

Thank you for your understanding and assistance in this matter.

Sincerely,

[Name]
[Title]

- **Be polite but firm.**

- **Indicate how you wish to continue a good working relationship.**

Path on CD-ROM: Customer service→Complaints from customer→Explaining→Explaining—example 2

Low product quality—as a customer

[DATE]

[Name]
[Company]
[Address]
[City, State ZIP]

Dear [   ]:

We recently ordered and received two picnic tables from your company and had them billed to our account.

When we received these tables, we discovered that the quality of their construction was not up to par with what we have come to expect from [Wood Lawn Tables, Inc.] The legs were not braced properly, the finish was missing in several areas and both of the tables had two bolts missing.

As previous customers of [Wood Lawn Table, Inc.] I must admit we were disappointed with the products. We would like either two replacement tables or our account credited [$550] for the two tables.

We appreciate your attention to this matter.

Sincerely,

[Name]
[Title]

- **Describe what is wrong with the item(s).**

- **Tell the company how you expect the problem to be solved.**

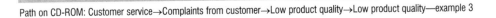

Path on CD-ROM: Customer service→Complaints from customer→Low product quality→Low product quality—example 3

Promise to check

[DATE]

[Name]
[Company]
[Address]
[City, State ZIP]

Dear [   ]:

I received your phone message [today] regarding the overdue bill for the [interior painting you did for us].

Thank you for letting us know we haven't paid you. I will check with the accounting department regarding the missing invoice.

Meanwhile, if you send a copy of the invoice and address it to me, I will personally deliver it to the accounting department and follow-up the next day to insure it was paid.

Let me know how I can be of further service to you.

Sincerely,

[Name]
[Title]

- **Acknowledge the problem.**

- **Explain how you are going to attempt to solve the problem.**

Path on CD-ROM: Customer service→Complaints from customer→Promise to check→Promise to check—example 1

Customer Appreciation

A letter thanking a customer for something he/she has done serves two purposes: it expresses thanks and gives the customer a good feeling about the company.

Points to remember when writing a letter thanking a customer for his/her actions:

- State the reason for the letter or memo.
- Explain how what the customer did helped the company or community.
- Demonstrate, through words, your appreciation for what the customer did.
- If appropriate, enclose a gift or invite the customer to an event.
- Thank the customer for his/her actions.

Example #1

[DATE]

[Name]
[Address]
[City, State ZIP]

Dear [   ]:

As a valued customer of [Bangs Department Store], we want you to know that we have appreciated your business over [the past year].

To show our appreciation, we have enclosed a special gift certificate worth [$10] off of your next purchase of any [fall or winter merchandise].

This certificate is our way of saying thank you for your patronage. Use it at the cash register or apply it to your next [Bangs'] credit card bill.

We look forward to serving you in the future.

Sincerely,

[Name]
[Title]

- **Acknowledge that the recipient is a valuable customer.**

- **Validate the letter's purpose with an enclosed gift.**

Path on CD-ROM: Customer service→Miscellaneous→Customer appreciation→Customer appreciation—example 1

CUSTOMER APPRECIATION

Example #2

[DATE]

[Name]
[Address]
[City, State ZIP]

Dear [   ]:

Four years ago, owning and operating a full-service Internet company was just a dream of mine. But, with perseverance, hard work and customers like you, that dream has become a reality.

Today, [WebWorks] has customers all over the globe and has developed Web pages for some well-recognized companies including [Olympus Card, Hot-Rod Motors and GenSport].

I couldn't have done it without the support and confidence of customers like you. Thank you for being our customer. We look forward to serving you again.

Sincerely,

[Name]
[Title]

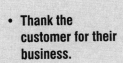

- **Thank the customer for their business.**

- **Encourage future business.**

Path on CD-ROM: Customer service→Gratitude→Customer→Customer—example 1

Example #3

[DATE]

[Name]
[Address]
[City, State ZIP]

Dear [   ]:

As we celebrate our [number] anniversary, we want to take this time to thank all of our customers whose loyal patronage has allowed us to be so successful over these past [number] of years.

Anniversaries cause us to reflect on the changes that have occurred since [company] first began business back in [year]. Our founder, [name], would be amazed at changes that have taken place, particularly the [modernization, the product selection] and the number of customers [company] has served. What has not changed over the years are the principles of honesty, quality and a fair price that [name] prided himself on.

Please stop in soon. Our new [spring] lines will be in the [showroom] on [date]. Bring this letter with you and receive a [amount] percent discount off of any purchase.

Sincerely,

[Name]
[Title]

- **Acknowledge the customer's loyalty and thank them for their business.**

- **Reference the discount if they show the letter and make a purchase.**

Path on CD-ROM: Customer service→Miscellaneous→Customer appreciation→Customer Appreciation—example 4

Customer Orders

Whenever you write a letter that either orders merchandise or refers to merchandise ordered, remember to:

- Specify the merchandise ordered. Use the exact name of the item and any other identifying information.
- Specify price per item and total order.
- Specify order number if available.

Whenever you have to inform a customer about bad news regarding their order, remember some of these helpful points:

- Start the letter with a positive or neutral buffer that buries the bad news before delivering it.
- Confirm the order.
- State the bad news and the reasons for it.
- Explain how the problem is being handled.
- Thank the customer and encourage future orders.

Back order

[DATE]

[Name]
[Company]
[Address]
[City, State ZIP]

Dear [   ]:

Thank you for your order of [300 miniature Chateau birdhouse kits].
Unfortunately, we are unable to fulfill your order at this time.

[Describe the reason for not being able to fulfill the order. Provide the customer with a possible new delivery date.]

I'm sorry for any inconvenience the delay may have caused. We will notify you
as soon as [we receive the hinges].

Sincerely,

[Name]
[Title]

- **Acknowledge the back order.**

- **Explain the reason for the back order.**

Path on CD-ROM: Customer service→Order→Notifying of back order→Notifying of back order—example 1

CUSTOMER ORDERS

Being processed

[DATE]

[Name]
[Company]
[Address]
[City, State ZIP]

Dear [   ]:

Thank you for selecting [IMPRINT T-SHIRTS] for your recent order. [IMPRINT T-SHIRTS counts among its customers the Squid, the new NFL expansion franchise.]

We are currently processing your order for [500 red, extra-large short-sleeve T-shirts with your logo imprinted in white across the front]. We expect your order to be ready [within the week] and we will call you when it is ready for pick-up.

[IMPRINT T-SHIRTS] appreciates your business.

Sincerely,

[Name]
[Title]

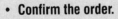

- **Confirm the order.**

- **Give an estimated date when the merchandise will be ready.**

Path on CD-ROM: Customer service→Order→Being processed→Being processed—example 1

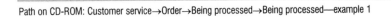

Decrease in price

FAX

TO: [   ]
FROM: [   ]
DATE: [   ]
SUBJECT: Price Decrease

Although we hesitate when we have to announce a price increase, with a price decrease there is no hesitation.

[We have negotiated a new contract with one of our suppliers. This contract was able to reduce the cost we pay for [material] by [amount].] This means we can pass along the savings directly to our customers.

We are reducing our [items] by [amount 2] percent effective [date]. The price decreases will be reflected [on the new price sheet that will be sent to you next week].

- Announce the price decrease and the reason behind it.

- Alert the reader to the price sheet that will be arriving.

Path on CD-ROM: Customer service→Order→Change in price-decrease→Change in price-decrease—example 3

Information

[DATE]

[Name/Title]
[Business/Organization Name]
[Address]
[City, State ZIP]

Dear [   ]:

Thank you for your interest in submissions to [*Coffee Growers Journal*]. As requested, you will find writers' guidelines enclosed. Your request for back issues was forwarded to our circulation department for processing. Please contact us if you have not received your issues in two to four weeks.

The guidelines outline what we require of our submissions, but there is one point we need to stress. When querying us, please put all ideas in writing. Include a detailed outline if possible and the names and telephone numbers of sources you plan to interview. Too many writers, especially new contributors, try to sell us story ideas over the telephone. It is too hard for us to evaluate the concept without seeing something in writing. It also indicates how much thought you have given the idea. The more complete your outline is, the more likely it is that we will use the story.

This does not extend to completed manuscripts, however, and we would caution you not to do a story on speculation. There is a good chance that we have covered the concept, or that we already have someone working on a similar story. A query with a detailed outline will let us decide if we are interested without causing you a lot of unnecessary work. Furthermore, we may see another story concept in the outline, making the final assignment into something completely different.

Please refer to the writers' guidelines for other limitations and opportunities. We look forward to hearing your thoughts and, we hope, seeing your byline in [*Coffee Growers Journal*].

Sincerely,

[Name]
[Title]

- **Acknowledge reader's request.**

- **Indicate what you are including in a brief summary.**

Path on CD-ROM: Customer service→Order→Info→Info—example 1

Initial order

[DATE]

[Name]
[Company]
[Address]
[City, State ZIP]

Dear [   ]:

Your order of [items] is being processed and will be shipped priority as you requested.

Thank you for trusting us to effectively handle your urgent order. We attempt to fulfill all orders, [not just the initial one] in an efficient and effective manner. We believe that our [prompt service and delivery] will encourage new customers to become repeat ones.

Let us know how we can help you further. We look forward to serving you again.

Sincerely,

[Name]
[Title]

- **Acknowledge the initial order.**

- **Thank the customer for his/her business and encourage repeat business.**

Path on CD-ROM: Customer service→Order→Initial order→Initial order—example 3

Insurance claim

[DATE]

[Name/Title]
[Business/Organization Name]
[Address]
[City, State ZIP]

Dear [   ]:

On [*date*], our company suffered a [*name or nature of mishap*] that damaged or destroyed [*approximate extent of damage, either in scope or financial approximation*]. This damage and loss is covered by your comprehensive business policy no. [*number of policy*].

[***Optional paragraph #1:*** *Detail the nature of the loss, including valuables and irreplaceables that may have been covered by the policy.*]

[***Optional paragraph #2:*** *Detail the business need for promptness, e.g., deadlines or payrolls to meet.*]

We need your immediate attention to this matter. A quick settlement will allow us to start the necessary restoration and once again begin serving our customers.

Thank you for your assistance.

Sincerely,

[Name]
[Title]

- **Indicate which policy covers the damage.**

- **Indicate why a speedy response is best for all parties.**

Path on CD-ROM: Customer service→Order→Insurance claim→Insurance claim—example 1

Large order

[DATE]

[Name]
[Company]
[Address]
[City, State ZIP]

Dear [   ]:

Your order of [date] really made our day. [When I routed it to our warehouse staff, they said it was the largest one of its kind to date.]

[When we stocked the [item], we had hoped that it would be popular. Your order confirmed our suspicions and has encouraged us to increase our reorder.]

We hope that the [item] proves a big hit with [your customers]. Let us know how we can assist you with any other needs.

Sincerely,

[Name]
[Title]

- **Acknowledge the large order.**

- **Encourage future business.**

Path on CD-ROM: Customer service→Order→Large order→Large order—example 4

CUSTOMER ORDERS

Ready for pick-up

[DATE]

[Name]
[Company]
[Address]
[City, State ZIP]

Dear [   ]:

We tried several times unsuccessfully to contact you by phone to notify you that the [pants] you purchased at [Finkle's Department Store have been altered] and are available for pick-up.

Please stop by the store some time [Monday through Saturday from 10 a.m. to 9 p.m. or Sunday from noon to 6 p.m.] to pick them up. They are being held at the returns desk in the back of the store.

You will need your receipt to claim your merchandise.

Thank you for shopping at [Finkle's].

Sincerely,

[Name]
[Title]

- Notify the customer that the item is ready for pick up.

- Inform the customer of the store's hours.

Path on CD-ROM: Customer service→Order→Merchandise ready for pick-up→Merchandise ready for pick-up—example 2

Sample

[DATE]

[Name/Title]
[Business/Organization Name]
[Address]
[City, State ZIP]

Dear [   ]:

We would like to order [two Minolta copiers (Product #36117)] as listed in your spring catalogue for [$1,832]. The copiers should be sent to:

> [Receiving Dept.]
> [Terrapin Industries]
> [3002 Industrial Dr.]
> [San Rafael, CA 96453]
> [Attn: Sam Johnson]

The invoice, with the product shipping date listed, should be sent to:

> [Accounting Dept.]
> [Attn: Gwen Hadley]
> [ACME Multiglomerate Inc.]
> [13761 Bonny Meadow Rd.]
> [Indianapolis, IN 45398]

We would appreciate a timely turnaround on this order. Ship via the normal common carrier your firm uses.

Thank you.

Sincerely,

[Name]
[Title]

- **Indicate product number and price.**

- **Clearly identify shipping address if different from invoice address.**

Path on CD-ROM: Customer service→Order→Order→Order—example 1

Miscellaneous

In this section we've included some letters for other areas of customer service that you may encounter that didn't fit into the other categories. Whatever the situation, always try to remember the basic principles for customer service letters:

- Even if the customer is wrong, present the subject matter in the most pleasant tone possible.
- Use a positive or neutral buffer when delivering negative news.
- Specify dates, prices, order numbers, invoice numbers, and any other data that will help you serve the customer.
- Always thank the customer for his/her business.
- Always encourage future business.

Cancel service

[DATE]

[Name]
[Address]
[City, State ZIP]

Dear [   ]:

This letter confirms that we have received your 30-day written request to terminate your [cable television service]. Your service was canceled on [June 30].

You will be billed for [cable service] for the month of [June]. Please remit the payment as you have previously.

If we can be of service in the future, please don't hesitate to contact us.

Sincerely,

[Name]
[Title]

- **Acknowledge the customer's request.**

- **Give the date the cancellation was effective.**

MISCELLANEOUS

Explanation of invoice

[DATE]

[Name]
[Address]
[City, State ZIP]

Dear [   ]:

I have enclosed a copy of our invoice for the [repair work done on your bathroom on July 8]. The invoice is for [$851], which includes [the installation of a new toilet, the removal of the old toilet and labor].

You will note that the invoice is [$15] more than the estimate. The extra [$15] is for [the landfill disposal fees for the old toilet].

Thank you for choosing [Edifice Remodelers. We do all the home improvement jobs you do not want to do.]

Sincerely,

[Name]
[Title]

- **Describe the contents of the envelope.**

- **Alert the reader to any changes on the invoice.**

Path on CD-ROM: Customer service→Transmittal→Invoice—explanation of fees→Invoice—explanation of fees—example 3

Explanation of payment

[DATE]

[Name]
[Company]
[Address]
[City, State ZIP]

Dear [   ]:

Enclosed please find our check [#425 for $1,987], which represents the first payment on our account. As we agreed upon, the remaining [$1,987] will be sent in [30 days].

Several of your products have been selling quite well. I'm particularly impressed with the [metal garden trellis – I've sold eight out of the 10 you shipped].

Thank you for extending us credit.

Sincerely,

[Name]
[Title]

- **Explain what the check is for and restate the credit terms.**

- **Letter provides a valuable record of the payment.**

Path on CD-ROM: Customer service→Transmittal→Payment on account→Payment on account—example 1

MISCELLANEOUS

Explanation of warranty

[DATE]

[Name]
[Address]
[City, State ZIP]

Dear [   ]:

Welcome to the family of [Quik-Vac vacuum cleaner] owners. When you bought a [Quik-Vac] you bought a [vacuum cleaner with a 90-year] reputation for quality and service.

With every [Quik-Vac vacuum cleaner] comes a [six-month] warranty, which covers parts and labor. Should your [vacuum cleaner] fail to perform to your satisfaction, simply take the machine into a [Quik-Vac certified repair shop]. They will fix it at no charge to you.

After the first [six months], you have the option of purchasing a service contract, which covers replacement parts for as long as you own the [vacuum cleaner]. I have enclosed a brochure explaining the details of the contract.

We hope you enjoy your new [vacuum cleaner].

Sincerely,

[Name]
[Title]

- **Explain the terms of the warranty.**

- **Offer the customer the option of extending the warranty.**

Path on CD-ROM: Customer service→Warranty→Terms→Terms—example 1

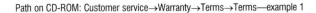

Honoring warranty

[DATE]

[Name]
[Address]
[City, State ZIP]

Dear [   ]:

Before a customer purchases a [Cut-Rite electric weed trimmer], each one is put through a rigorous screening to ensure that the machine is reliable and dependable. We are so confident of our quality that our warranties run for as long as the customer owns the product.

I have routed your letter of [June 4] informing us of a problem with the [trimmer] to our production department. They will review manufacturing procedures to identify potential problem areas.

We apologize for your inconvenience. Simply send us the bill for the repairs and we will reimburse you for the costs.

Should you ever experience another problem with this or any of our other [electric tools] simply take the product to your nearest [Cut-Rite dealer] who will repair it at no cost to you.

Sincerely,

[Name]
[Title]

- **Explain the warranty.**

- **Tell the customer how you will honor the warranty.**

Path on CD-ROM: Customer service→Warranty→Honoring→Honoring—example 1

MISCELLANEOUS

Recommending an additional warranty

[DATE]

[Name]
[Address]
[City, State ZIP]

Dear [   ]:

We hope you are enjoying your new [item]. When you purchased that [item] you automatically received a [amount of time] warranty on all parts and labor.

We would like to encourage you to purchase an extended warranty, which covers the [item] for as long as you own it. The additional warranty costs [amount] and will provide blanket coverage as long as you own the [item].

Enclosed is a brochure describing the extended warranty. Please take a moment to review it and consider how much you depend on your [item]. Isn't [amount 1] per day a small price to pay for peace of mind?

We hope you will take advantage of this added benefit. Thank you for purchasing a [item].

Sincerely,

[Name]
[Title]

- **Explain the reason for the letter and why the reader should take advantage of your offer.**

- **Break the price down into a per/day cost to help avoid "sticker shock."**

Path on CD-ROM: Customer service→Warranty→Recommending an additional warranty→Recommending an additional warranty—example 1

Refusal of a request for more information

[DATE]

[Name/Title]
[Business/Organization Name]
[Address]
[City, State ZIP]

Dear [   ]:

We have received your request for [more information regarding access to specific procedures regarding bank overdrafts in general, and your account information in particular. A printout of your recent activity is enclosed.]

Unfortunately, beyond general procedures, company policy prohibits us from providing more detailed information. [This is considered strategic information and may not be revealed except to the bank's executives.]

We are sorry we could not be more helpful. If you would like to pursue the matter further, please contact [*name*], operations manager. If you have any specific requests regarding other aspects of operations, you may also contact [*name*].

Thank you for your inquiry and continued patronage.

With best wishes,

[Name]
[Title]

- **Acknowledge receipt of request.**

- **Indicate why you cannot divulge the information.**

Path on CD-ROM: Customer service→Customer requests→Information→Information—example 5

Refusing to honor warranty

[DATE]

[Name]
[Address]
[City, State ZIP]

Dear [   ]:

Thank you for bringing to our attention the problems you had with [five of our liquid crystal display units]. Our quality control department is currently testing the ones you returned for possible defects.

All of our units come with a full [one-year] warranty. [Premier LCD] stands behind all of our products, but a check of our records finds that your displays were installed [twenty-three] months ago. Because more than a year has passed, [Premier LCD] cannot reimburse you for the cost of the displays as you had requested.

We look forward to serving you in the future.

Sincerely,

[Name]
[Title]

- **Restate terms of the warranty.**

- **Explain why the company will not honor the warranty.**

Path on CD-ROM: Customer service→Warranty→Refuse to honor for cause→Refuse to honor for cause—example 1

Request for customer feedback

[DATE]

[Name]
[Company]
[Address]
[City, State ZIP]

Dear [   ]:

Customer feedback is important to us. That is why I am interested in hearing your comments about the [dinner that we catered for your sales staff last week].

Although things seemed to have gone smoothly from our standpoint, the customer's view of the [service and food quality] is what is critical.

I know you are very busy, but I have a small favor to ask of you. Would you please complete and return the short survey at the bottom of the letter? I have included a postage-paid envelope for your convenience.

We look forward to your response and thank you for your business.

Sincerely,

[Name]
[Title]

- **Thank the customer for his/her business.**

- **Make it convenient for the customer to respond by including a postage-paid envelope.**

Path on CD-ROM: Customer service→Miscellaneous→Follow up after services have been rendered→Follow up after services have been rendered—example 2

[DATE]

[Name/Title]
[Business/Organization Name]
[Address]
[City, State ZIP]

Dear [   ]:

Thank you for your recent inquiry. Enclosed you will find the information requested on [*subject*] from [*source of material*].

We have received numerous requests for this information, which has led us to explore other facets of [*subject*] and related topics. If you would like further information as we find it, please return the enclosed postcard with your name and address written on the back. We will keep you on our mailing list for future information.

Thanks for your interest and thanks for reading!

Best regards,

[Name]
[Title]

- **Acknowledge receipt of inquiry.**

- **Indicate what you are including.**

Path on CD-ROM: Customer service→Customer requests→Information→Information—example 3

MISCELLANEOUS

Welcome to new customer

[DATE]

[Name]
[Address]
[City, State ZIP]

Dear [   ]:

Welcome to the [Mega Bank] family. New customers give us a reason to celebrate.

Our goal is personalized service for every customer. The enclosed card lists your account number and the name of your customer service representative. If you have a concern or a complaint, simply call the number and you will be linked to your representative who will be glad to answer your questions and ensure you're satisfied with your treatment at [Mega Bank].

Thank you for choosing [Mega Bank].

Sincerely,

[Name]
[Title]

- **Welcome new customer.**

- **Describe benefits of being a customer.**

Path on CD-ROM: Customer service→Welcome to new customer→Welcome to new customer—example 1

Payments

When writing a letter about payment issues as the customer, it's always good to be up front with your suppliers. For example, if you're writing about why a payment was late, explain what happened and how you're handling the matter to prevent it from happening again.

When writing letters to customers about their payment issues, be unfailingly courteous. In many cases the letter is in response to a problem and your courteous tone will help keep the customer's goodwill. Letters in response to payments from customers should:

- Acknowledge the payment, the amount and type of payment vehicle—cash, check, or charge.
- Thank the customer for the payment.
- State the problem with the payment.
- Identify any discrepancies between what is owed and the amount paid.
- Explain how you would like the problem solved.
- Ask the customer to solve the problem.
- Encourage future business.

PAYMENTS

Acknowledgement

[DATE]

[Name]
[Address]
[City, State ZIP]

Dear [   ]:

Thank you for your payment of [October 2 for $456.87]. We hope that you are enjoying your new [Fast Heat electric stove].

It is customers like you that have helped make [Sam's Appliance the appliance leader in Cantonsville for over 25 years].

We appreciate your patronage and look forward to serving you again.

Sincerely,

[Name]
[Title]

- **Acknowledge the payment and the amount.**

- **Thank the customer for his/her business.**

Path on CD-ROM: Customer service→Payment from customer→Acknowledge→Acknowledge—example 3

Apology for incorrect payment

[DATE]

[Name]
[Company]
[Address]
[City, State ZIP]

Dear [   ]:

I have enclosed our check [#3256 for $456.17] to cover the remaining balance on our account.

The check covers the underpayment of invoice [#78452 last month]. The correct amount was inadvertently transposed when printing the check.

Please accept my apologies for the mistake.

Sincerely,

[Name]
[Title]

- **Acknowledge the mistake and offer an apology.**

- **Explain which invoice the check covers.**

Path on CD-ROM: Customer service→Order→Apology for incorrect payment→Apology for incorrect payment—example 1

Close an account

[DATE]

[Name]
[Address]
[City, State ZIP]

Dear [   ]:

With the receipt of your check [#456 for $35.62], your account has a zero balance.

As you requested in your letter that accompanied your check, we have closed account [#5555-4444].

Please do not hesitate to contact us if we may be of service in the future.

Sincerely,

[Name]
[Title]

- **Acknowledge the customer's check and letter.**

- **Explain that you have honored the customer's request to close the account.**

Path on CD-ROM: Customer service→Payment from customer→Close account→Close account—example 1

Discount for early payment

[DATE]

[Name]
[Address]
[City, State ZIP]

Dear [   ]:

We appreciate the fine way you have paid your bill. Because of your record of prompt payment we have applied a [5%] discount to your [Fidelity Department Store charge card bill].

During this quarter only, if you charge [$100] or more to your account and pay the bill within [10] days of receiving the statement, we will apply a [5%] discount to your purchases.

[Fidelity] appreciates your patronage and looks forward to serving all of your [fashion] needs.

Sincerely,

[Name]
[Title]

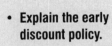

- **Explain the early discount policy.**

- **Encourage the customer to use it.**

Path on CD-ROM: Customer service→Payment from customer→Discount for early payment→Discount for early payment—example 5

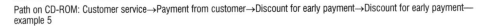

Expired credit card

[DATE]

[Name]
[Address]
[City, State ZIP]

Dear [   ]:

On [July 3] you ordered a [refrigerator] and asked us to bill your credit card. However, we are unable to finish processing your order because the card has a [July] expiration date. Please submit another credit card or a check for the entire amount.

As soon as we receive payment we will ship [your merchandise].

Thank you for your order.

Sincerely,

[Name]
[Title]

- **Explain the problem with the card.**

- **Ask customer to provide another source of payment.**

Path on CD-ROM: Customer service→Customer payments→Expired credit card→Expired credit card—example 1

Explanation for late payment

[DATE]

[Name]
[Address]
[City, State ZIP]

Dear [   ]:

As a customer who has always prided himself on paying his bills on time, writing this letter is one of the most difficult things I've had to do.

The [loss of our primary customer last month has caused us to close down two lines]. [Until we obtain another customer], our cash flow will be very erratic. My primary focus is on keeping the business open, but I need your help. Would you be willing to [modify your credit terms from 75% due upon receipt of the merchandise to 50% and extend the payment deadline from net 30 to net 60]?

Our top priority is [replacing our lost customer] and returning to our original payment schedule.

We appreciate your consideration of this matter.

Sincerely,

[Name]
[Title]

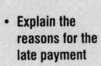

- Explain the reasons for the late payment

- Ask for an extension in paying your account.

Path on CD-ROM: Customer service→Payment from customer→Explanation for late payment→Explanation for late payment—example 4

304

PAYMENTS

Invalid credit card number

[DATE]

[Name]
[Address]
[City, State ZIP]

Dear [   ]:

On [February 8] you placed a phone order for [two tickets to the Slamm'n concert]. Unfortunately, the credit card number you provided was invalid.

We are currently holding your [tickets]. Please submit another credit card or a check for the [$57 by March 1] or we will release the tickets.

Sincerely,

[Name]
[Title]

- **Explain the problem.**

- **State what you want the customer to do in order to solve the problem.**

Path on CD-ROM: Customer service→Payment from customer→Invalid card number→Invalid card number—example 1

PAYMENTS

Partial payment

[DATE]

[Name]
[Address]
[City, State ZIP]

Dear [   ]:

Thank you for your partial payment of [$6,500]. We have applied it to your account and the current balance is now [$11,436].

The remaining amount is due [February 15]. If you anticipate a problem with this, please contact me for alternative payment arrangements.

Your business is very important to us. Let us know if we can be of service.

Sincerely,

[Name]
[Title]

- **Acknowledge the payment and the remaining balance.**

- **Remind customer of the due date of his/her next payment.**

Path on CD-ROM: Customer service→Payment from customer→Partial payment→Partial payment—example 4

Postdated checks

[DATE]

[Name]
[Company]
[Address]
[City, State ZIP]

Dear [   ]:

We received your check [#44567] for [invoice #AG-457-98 for 12 cases of Round-the-Clock Coffee]. The check has been postdated by [one week].

In the past we have accommodated postdated checks. But [higher banking fees] prevent us from accepting this kind of payment.

Because you are a valued customer of [Coffee World], we will make an exception in this case. However, in the future we will be unable to honor any checks without the current date.

We appreciate your business and your cooperation.

Sincerely,

[Name]
[Title]

- **Acknowledge the order and the postdated check.**

- **Explain your policy on postdated checks and why it is necessary.**

Path on CD-ROM: Customer service→Payment from customer→Postdated checks→Postdated checks—example 1

PAYMENTS

Over credit card limit

[DATE]

[Name]
[Address]
[City, State ZIP]

Dear [   ]:

[Three] times over the past [12 months] you have presented your credit card for payment on your account and our credit card processor has rejected it for insufficient funds. As a result we are canceling your account with us.

We regret we must take this step, but it costs us time and money to continuously contact you for alternative methods of payment.

We welcome your business as a cash customer and encourage you to reapply for a credit account with us after six months.

Sincerely,

[Name]
[Title]

- **Acknowledge the problem and be specific about why you are canceling the account.**

- **Encourage future business on a cash basis.**

Path on CD-ROM: Customer service→Customer payments→Over credit card limit→Over credit card limit—example 4

Requesting further information

[DATE]

[Name]
[Address]
[City, State ZIP]

Dear [   ]:

We received your check dated [March 11] for the amount of [$45.79]. In reviewing our accounts, we have discovered we have no record of any order from you.

Are our records correct? If our records are incorrect, would you send us a copy of the bill? If you sent the check to us in error, we will gladly return it to you.

Please notify us of your decision.

Thank you.

Sincerely,

[Name]
[Title]

- **Acknowledge the payment and explain the problem.**

- **Ask the customer what he/she would like done with the check.**

Path on CD-ROM: Customer service→Customer payments→Requesting further information→Requesting further information—example 1

PAYMENTS

Underpayment

[DATE]

[Name/Title]
[Business/Organization Name]
[Address]
[City, State ZIP]

Dear [   ]:

Nobody's perfect. We here at [Discount Motors know that as well as the next person, and we are sure your error in the order and prepayment for the Baby Moon hubcaps for your vintage '57 Chevrolet Bel Air] was unintentional.

[We realized only after the fact that the catalogue and price that you showed to [*name*] in the parts department, was actually that of a competitor, Hi-Power Auto Sales. When we checked the order, we found that the price in our most recent catalogue was actually 15 percent higher than the price you prepaid [*name*] before ordering.]

We're sorry for the mix-up, but we're happy to tell you that your [Baby Moons] have arrived. If you will pay [*name*] the difference between the actual price and what you paid, he will be happy to install them personally.

Yours in motoring,

[Name]
[Title]

- **Start with a neutral buffer.**

- **Explain the mix-up and how you'd like to resolve the matter.**

Path on CD-ROM: Customer service→Customer payments→Underpayment→Underpayment—example 1

Policies

Letters notifying customers of new policies or changes to old ones can either bring good news or bad news depending upon the customer's perspective. If the policy is apt to bring dissatisfaction, be sure to stress heavily the benefits of the policy to the customer. Remember to:

- State the existing policy, change in policy, or new policy as appropriate.
- Explain why any changes were initiated.
- Explain how the policy benefits the customer.
- Give the customer a name and phone number to call for questions.
- Thank the customer for his/her business.
- Encourage future business.

POLICIES

Announcement

[DATE]

[Name/Title]
[Business/Organization Name]
[Address]
[City, State ZIP]

Dear [   ]:

Communication is important to any business, and we wanted you to be among the first to know that as of [*date of announcement's effectiveness*], [*name of firm*] [*purpose of announcement*].

[***Optional paragraph 1:*** *Explain the rationale for the change, highlighting those characteristics affecting the letter recipient's company.*]

[***Optional paragraph 2:*** *Explain how the change will better improve service to or the relationship with the letter recipient's company.*]

If you have any questions at all about [*description of change*], feel free to contact me at [*address and/or telephone number*]. Your relationship with our firm is important, and we hope that this change will only enhance the work we have already begun together.

Very best regards,

[Name]
[Title]

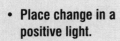

- **Place change in a positive light.**

- **Encourage a positive working relationship and future business.**

Path on CD-ROM: Customer service→Customer policy→Change→Change—example 1

Change in policy

[DATE]

[Name]
[Company]
[Address]
[City, State ZIP]

Dear [   ]:

[Justin Industries] is going smoke-free. As of [September 18] there will be no smoking inside the buildings or on the grounds of [Justin Industries].

We believe that this change will improve the health and environmental quality of [Justin Industries'] employees, suppliers, and customers. Suppliers and customers are asked to extinguish all smoking materials before entering the facility.

Sincerely,

[Name]
[Title]

- **Explain the new policy and benefits.**

- **Give effective date.**

Path on CD-ROM: Customer service→New→New—example 1

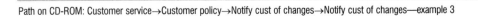

New policy

[DATE]

[Name]
[Address]
[City, State ZIP]

Dear [   ]:

An audit of our returns found that the majority of [Cornwell Glass] products were rejected because of breakage during shipping. After reviewing our options, [Cornwell Glass] has decided to adopt a new shipping policy.

Effective [November 15, Cornwell Glass] will be using [Rush Freight] as a carrier. We will also begin packing all of our breakable products in Styrofoam boxes to insure that the products you order arrive intact.

These two changes should further improve the quality of the [Cornwell Glass] products you receive.

Sincerely,

[Name]
[Title]

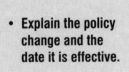

- Explain the policy change and the date it is effective.

- Point out the benefits of the change for the customer.

Path on CD-ROM: Customer service→Customer policy→Notify cust of changes→Notify cust of changes—example 3

Reminder

[DATE]

[Name]
[Company]
[Address]
[City, State ZIP]

Dear [   ]:

Several recent incidents of unauthorized returns lead us to believe that many of our customers are confused about the new returns policy.

Effective [September 1, Captain's Cutlery] will not accept any returns for credit or refund without prior permission. If there is a problem with your order and you want to return it for a refund or credit, call our shipping department for instructions before arranging transportation.

Questions about this policy can be directed to me at [555-9090].

[Captain's Cutlery] appreciates your business.

Sincerely,

[Name]
[Title]

- **Restate new refund policy.**

- **Keep lines of communication open by providing a phone number for questions.**

Path on CD-ROM: Customer service→Customer policy→Reminder→Reminder—example 1

Problems

Letters written to customers in response to problems that were brought to your attention must be sincere, offer to help solve the problem and attempt to retain the customer's goodwill. A satisfied customer will tell only a few people that he/she is satisfied. A dissatisfied customer will tell 10 to 20 people about their unhappiness with a product, company, or service. When writing letters to customers in response to a problem, remember to:

- Acknowledge the correspondence or phone call that prompted the letter.
- Explain the reason for the letter.
- Restate the problem—include details such as a description of the item, cost, purchase date, invoice number.
- Explain why the problem happened if known.
- Apologize for the problem.
- Explain what you or the company will do to solve the problem—e.g., exchange the item, offer a refund or credit, pay for the repairs, etc.
- If you tell the customer that you will follow up with him/her, make certain that you do it.
- Thank the customer for his/her business.
- Encourage future business.

Apology for inappropriate collection letter

[DATE]

[Name]
[Address]
[City, State ZIP]

Dear [   ]:

Our faces are red. We really made a big mistake when we sent your file to our collection agency.

Let me explain how it happened. We have two customers with your name. The only difference is the middle initial. Our accounts receivable department mistakenly routed the wrong account to the [name] collection agency.

I have notified both our accounts receivable department and the [name] collection agency of this matter. Your account will be cleared and a note will be placed in your file explaining the problem.

We are deeply embarrassed about this incident. Your record of prompt payments puts you among our most valued customers. We hope this situation did not damage our good relationship.

Sincerely,

[Name]
[Title]

- **Acknowledge the error and explain the reason behind it.**

- **Explain how the error was resolved.**

Path on CD-ROM: Customer service→Customer problems→Apology for inappropriate collection letter→Apology for inappropriate collection letter—example 4

PROBLEMS

Billing error

[DATE]

[Name/Title]
[Business/Organization Name]
[Address]
[City, State ZIP]

Dear [   ]:

Your recent bill of [$142.32] mystifies us. Surely past telephone bills indicate that we make frequent calls to [Maine, Florida, and Oklahoma]. But we are at a loss to explain three successive calls to [Taipei, Taiwan and four calls to Sydney, Australia] on [May 6 and 8, respectively].

Rest assured no one in this house made them. We can only consider them another instance of computer error or, perhaps, fraud. Whatever the reason, we would like them removed from our bill. Our enclosed check does not include payment for these charges.

Thanks for your attention to this matter.

Best regards,

[Name]

- **Detail which items you are disputing.**

- **Indicate the steps you are taking.**

Path on CD-ROM: Customer service→Customer problems→Error→Error—example 1

Mistake in invoice

[DATE]

[Name]
[Company]
[Address]
[City, State ZIP]

Dear [   ]:

We just received an invoice for [$2576 dated April 5 for a swimming pool heating unit].

We believe the bill to be in error. In reviewing our purchase order [#55432] and our warehouse records, we find we ordered and received the [1500 BTU model], not the [2700 BTU model]. The bill reflects the price for the 2700 BTU model.

Please correct your records and send us a new bill for [$2056, the price of the 1500 BTU model].

Thank you.

Sincerely,

[Name]
[Title]

- **Describe the potential error and why you believe it to be an error.**

- **Offer a satisfactory solution to the problem.**

Path on CD-ROM: Customer service→Customer problems→Mistake in invoice→Mistake in invoice—example 1

PROBLEMS

Mix-up

[DATE]

[Name/Title]
[Business/Organization Name]
[Address]
[City, State ZIP]

Dear [   ]:

Please accept our apology in the mix-up over your recent [chair] purchase. You were right and our billing department was wrong. They lost the sales file on this purchase and reverted to basic procedure for the item. The delivery man was only doing what he was instructed to do in such situations.

By now your [chair] should have been returned to you and the account settled. If that hasn't happened, please call me immediately and I will see to the delivery personally. There is no excuse for any further mix-up.

By way of restitution, please accept this coupon for 15% off your next [furniture] purchase. [This coupon will be honored for all full- and sale-priced items except spas and hot tubs, which we subcontract from another distributor. We also have added you to our Customer Gold list, which will enable you to preview all items prior to their going on advertised sale.]

Again, please accept our apology for this mix-up. We thank you for your continued business.

Warm regards,

[Name]
[Title]

- **Explain what happened.**

- **Offer restitution to encourage future business.**

Path on CD-ROM: Customer service→Customer problems→Allowing return for refund→Allowing return for refund—example 1

Payment adjustment

[DATE]

[Name]
[Address]
[City, State ZIP]

Dear [   ]:

Thank you for contacting us regarding your account.

We received your payment on [July 28]. Your payment was not credited to your account because we received it after the statement had been generated. You will see the [July 28] payment reflected on your next statement.

Because we received the payment after we had generated the statement, you will also see a finance charge assessed to your account. I have reversed this finance charge for you, which will appear on your next statement.

If you have further questions about your account, please do not hesitate to call.

Sincerely,

[Name]
[Title]

- **Acknowledge the problem.**

- **Explain the adjustment that will solve the problem.**

Path on CD-ROM: Customer service→Customer problems→Adjusting accounts→Adjusting accounts—example 1

Response to an error

[DATE]

[Name]
[Company]
[Address]
[City, State ZIP]

Dear [   ]:

Did you ever have one of those days where nothing goes right? [February 9] was one of those days for the [Seeman Company]. A power surge knocked out our computer system. When the system came back up, we discovered we had a number of corrupted files.

One of those corrupted files was the accounts receivable file. We realized later that all of the invoices we mailed on [February 10 and 11] were inaccurate, including the one you received on [February 15].

We have since adjusted all the accounts and sent out new invoices. Because of the inconvenience to our customers, we have enclosed a 10% off coupon good on your next order.

We appreciate your patience during this time and look forward to serving you again.

Sincerely,

[Name]
[Title]

- **Acknowledge the problem and explain how the problem occurred.**

- **Explain the solution and thank the customer for his/her patience.**

Path on CD-ROM: Customer service→Customer problems→Response to invoice error→Response to invoice error—example 1

Returns

Customer returns letters authorize the customer to return merchandise to you. They also explain your policy on returns and how you are going to credit the customer's account for the returned merchandise. Letters that accept returns should:

- Acknowledge the customer's request to return the merchandise.
- Describe the merchandise including amount, price, size, and color if applicable.
- Affirm that you will accept the returned merchandise.
- State how the return will be handled, whether it's an exchange, refund, or store credit.
- Thank the customer for his/her business.
- Encourage future business.

Letters that refuse to accept back merchandise should:

- Begin with a neutral or positive buffer to bury the negative news.
- Acknowledge the request to return merchandise.
- Describe the merchandise including amount, price, size, and color if applicable.
- State the company's return policy.
- State tactfully, but firmly, that you are refusing to allow the customer to return the merchandise for exchange, refund, or credit.
- Give a reason for the refusal.
- Thank the customer for his/her business.
- Encourage future business.

RETURNS

Accept for credit

[DATE]

[Name]
[Address]
[City, State ZIP]

Dear [   ]:

We are sorry to hear of your disappointment with our [clear plastic folders]. Customer satisfaction is [Crystal Plastic's] number one goal.

We feel so strongly about that goal that if any of our products does not meet your expectations, you may return them for a full refund.

Your account has been credited [$87.50] for the returned [folders]. You will see the amount reflected in your next bill.

Sincerely,

[Name]
[Title]

- **Acknowledge the return and explain the policy.**

- **Encourage future business.**

Path on CD-ROM: Customer service→Customer returns→Accept for credit→Accept for credit—example 1

Apology for unauthorized return

[DATE]

[Name]
[Company]
[Address]
[City, State ZIP]

Dear [   ]:

When [company] makes a mistake, we make a big one. On [date] we returned [amount] of [product] without your authorization. We unintentionally neglected that step despite having previous experience with returning products to you.

We sincerely apologize for this error and appreciate your willingness to bend the rules for us. Since [date], we have instituted [a pre-printed checklist for our warehouse clerks to use when returning merchandise]. [On your form the words "Call for Authorization" are printed in red.]

Thank you for your understanding and patience.

Sincerely,

[Name]
[Title]

- **Explain the situation and the cause.**

- **Describe any steps you have taken to prevent the problem from recurring.**

Path on CD-ROM: Customer service→Customer returns→Apology for unauthorized return→Apology for unauthorized return—example 3

325

RETURNS

Duplicate order

[DATE]

[Name]
[Address]
[City, State ZIP]

Dear [   ]:

[World of Herbs] appreciates your recent order. In reviewing our accounts, we discovered that we made an error on your order and shipped you two cases of [Vim'nVigor Vitamins] instead of the one you requested.

We apologize for this error and any inconvenience it may have caused you. Please call our Customer Service department to arrange shipment of the second case. I have enclosed a postage-paid address label for return via the U.S. Postal Service and a [Return Merchandise Authorization sticker should you choose to use UPS].

We apologize for our error and thank you for your understanding. [World of Herbs] counts you as a valued customer.

Sincerely,

[Name]
[Title]

- **Explain problem with order.**

- **Request return of merchandise and assume customer will honor the request.**

Path on CD-ROM: Customer service→Customer returns→Duplicate order→Duplicate order—example 1

Exchange

[DATE]

[Name]
[Address]
[City, State ZIP]

Dear [   ]:

We are very sorry to hear that the lawnmower part you ordered did not fit your lawnmower. We will be happy to exchange it for the right part.

Simply bring your purchase to any [Cut-Rite] lawnmower dealer along with the model and make of your lawnmower and they will help you choose the right part.

We thank you for thinking of [Cut-Rite] tools for all your lawn and garden needs.

Sincerely,

[Name]
[Title]

- **Acknowledge the problem.**

- **Explain to customer that he/she can exchange the part for a new one.**

Path on CD-ROM: Customer service→Customer returns→Exchange→Exchange—example 1

RETURNS

[DATE]

[Name]
[Address]
[City, State ZIP]

Dear [   ]:

Recently you returned a [Hi-Pro fan (model # 7B-451-98)] to our company. Although the box was marked "returns," we did not find any written instructions included with the merchandise.

In order to process this return, we need additional information. You may complete and return the enclosed form or call our customer service department between [8 a.m. and 5 p.m. CST] to provide the missing information. If you call, please reference the file number: [#67-342].

Thank you for choosing a [Hi-Pro product].

Sincerely,

[Name]
[Title]

- **Acknowledge receipt of product.**

- **Request additional information so you can properly process the return.**

Path on CD-ROM: Customer service→Customer returns→Need more information→Need more information—example 1

Unauthorized return

[DATE]

[Name]
[Company]
[Address]
[City, State ZIP]

Dear [   ]:

Your correspondence of [April 5] inquired about a refund for the [two cases of calligraphy pens] you returned.

Unfortunately, because the return was unauthorized, we cannot give you credit for the [pens]. Our returns policy states that merchandise must have malfunctioned or been damaged before we will grant a refund or a credit. Ordering too many of one item does not constitute a reason for either.

Because of your long history with us, we are willing, however, to exchange the [pens] for another item of equal or lesser value.

Let us know how you want this matter handled. Customer satisfaction is important to us.

Sincerely,

[Name]
[Title]

- **Explain returns policy and why this return was unauthorized.**

- **Make an exception if the situation warrants it.**

Path on CD-ROM: Customer service→Customer returns→Unauthorized→Unauthorized—example 1

Human Resources

Data and people. These two sometimes contradictory things are key elements in human resources writing. Data means records. Often when writing human resources letters and memos, you will consult "data" before writing. These data might include attendance records, pension payouts, or length of employment. Data is what makes human resources writing credible. Don't write without it.

At the same time, human resources letters and memos are written for real people who have families and feelings. Your human resources correspondence need not be as jazzy as sales or marketing letters. It does, however, need to express concern and caring for employees. Keeping people in mind means having a heart.

Special note: Many human resources letters have many legal implications. The letters in this product are samples for consideration only; laws may have changed since their writing. In addition these sample letters cannot be exactly right for your company's situation without adapting them. Please consult with your attorney about your specific situation.

Accepting a job offer

[DATE]

[Name]
[Address]
[City, State ZIP]

Dear [   ]:

It's a pleasure to accept your offer of the [radiology technician] position at the salary of [$22,000] a year.

I'm enclosing the benefits paperwork you asked me to review and sign. As we discussed on the phone earlier, I have already spoken with my current employer and will be able to start on [May 22].

I'm very enthusiastic about my new position with [ABC Inc.] Thank you for offering me this challenging opportunity.

Sincerely,

[Name]
[Title]

- **Confirm your acceptance, naming the position, the agreed-upon salary, and start date.**

- **Show your enthusiasm about taking the position.**

Path on CD-ROM: Human resources→Hiring→Accepting a job offer→Accepting a job offer—example 1

Accepting training

TO: [   ]
FROM: [   ]
DATE: [   ]
SUBJECT: Approving your stress seminar

The stress seminar sounds like a great idea—timely, not too expensive, and something you can share afterwards with staff.

Please let me know the exact date of the seminar so I can help cover for you in your absence.

- **Compliment the requester's choice.**

- **Address any details that haven't already been covered.**

Path on CD-ROM: Human resources→Human resources→Accepting training→Accepting training—example 1

Acknowledging receipt of a resume

[DATE]

[Name]
[Title]
[Company]
[Address]
[City, State ZIP]

Dear [   ]:

Thank you for your interest in the open [librarian] position. We will be collecting resumes until [the end of the month], and conducting interviews with our top candidates by [the week of the 8].

We will call within two weeks if we would like to arrange an interview with you. Thanks again for applying.

Sincerely,

[Name]
[Title]

- **Explain in general terms the hiring process that will be followed.**

- **Thank the candidate for his or her interest.**

Path on CD-ROM: Human resources→Hiring→Acknowledging receipt of resume→Acknowledging receipt of resume—example 1

Addressing a potential conflict of interest

INTEROFFICE MEMORANDUM

TO: [   ]
FROM: [   ]
DATE: [   ]
SUBJECT: [Conflict of interest]

[Smith, Gefske and Taylor Attorneys] has the interests of its clients at heart. That's why we cannot allow our employees to share information with companies that compete with our clients.

I recently learned that your affiliation with [Beauty at Home Inc.] may be in conflict with our work serving [Gorgeous Girl Cosmetics]. Having a conflict of interest is serious and could jeopardize your continued employment with [Smith, Gefske and Taylor]. By the end of the week, please write me a memo explaining the nature of your affiliation with [Beauty at Home].

I hope we can find a mutually agreeable solution for this situation.

- Identify the alleged conflict of interest.

- Give the employee time to respond before taking any action.

Path on CD-ROM: Human resources→Employee relations→Addressing potential conflict of interest→Addressing potential conflict of interest—example 1

336

Announcing a weight-loss program

INTEROFFICE MEMORANDUM

TO: [   ]
FROM: [   ]
DATE: [   ]
SUBJECT: Weight loss program starts [date]

What can we do to help?

That was the opening question we asked on our recent employee survey.
"Provide a weight-loss program" was so often suggested, we've contracted
with [group] to provide this benefit to you.

The program will be held on [number of weeks] [day]s from [times] in the
[where] starting [date]. The format will be [describe presentation]. Each class
costs [amount], payable to the instructor when you attend a session.

If you are interested in participating, please let [name] know by [date]. If there
are other programs you'd like us to consider offering, please let us know!

- Show how the
  program is
  another employee
  benefit.

- Ask for an RSVP
  by a certain date
  so you'll know
  how many will be
  attending.

Applying for a job

DATE

[Name]
[Company]
[Address]
[City, State ZIP]

Dear [   ]:

If you want to hire a manager who knows how to work with people, knows hotel management like the back of his hand, and knows what it takes to be a team player, you might just want to hire me.

I moved up through the ranks of hotel management while in high school. I answered the phones, supervised the front desk and, eventually, decided hotel management was for me. As you can see from the enclosed resume, [I now have a degree and six years of experience managing hotels in medium-sized markets].

[Franklin Inn's] policy that allows managers to keep learning and move up would really motivate me to keep performing at a high level. You'd find me a valuable employee now, and an increasingly valuable one in the future.

Do you have any positions opening up in the next few months? I'd be happy to come in at your convenience to discuss your staffing needs and my qualifications. I will phone you early next week to see if a meeting would be possible.

Thank you for your consideration.

Sincerely,

[Name]

- Use a catchy lead-in, as the potential employer didn't ask you to send this letter.

- Showing knowledge of the company is often advantageous.

Path on CD-ROM: Human resources→Employment→Applying for job (unsolicited)→Applying for job (unsolicited)—example 1

Asking for job advice

[DATE]

[Name]
[Address]
[City, State ZIP]

Dear [   ]:

As a student at [university], I have studied hard, made good grades and tried to participate in extracurricular activities that would boost my leadership skills. What I feel I am lacking is real insight into just what employers need from an employee in my field.

Would you be willing to give me a good steer? As an employer of [profession], you must see a lot of good resumes. Would you take a look at mine and let me know how I can strengthen my application? I will take your advice very seriously.

Thank you for your time and consideration.

Sincerely,

[Name]
[Title]

- **Use this technique to introduce yourself to potential employers before an actual job solicitation.**

- **Give the employer an opportunity to state his or her needs.**

Path on CD-ROM: Human resources→Employment→Asking for job advice from potential employer→Asking for job advice from potential employer—example 1

Declining a job offer

[DATE]

[Name]
[Address]
[City, State ZIP]

Dear [   ]:

Thank you so much for taking the time to talk with me last week. The [Butler Schools] are doing some fantastic work with young people.

At the same time I applied to [Butler], I also applied to several other schools, all leaders in education. Because one of the others has offered me a position working with 4th graders, the age group that is my special area of interest, I have accepted the other school's offer.

Thanks again for meeting with me. I really enjoyed meeting you and appreciate your consideration.

Sincerely,

[Name]
[Title]

- **Use a "buffer" in the opening paragraph that makes it easier to hear the bad news that you are declining the offer.**

- **Find a tactful way to explain why you are accepting another offer.**

Path on CD-ROM: Human resources→Hiring→Declining a job offer→Declining a job offer—example 1

Discrimination and harassment

INTEROFFICE MEMORANDUM

TO: [   ]
FROM: [   ]
DATE: [   ]
SUBJECT: [Discrimination and harassment]

In this country, our rights to do something are limited when, by doing it, we infringe on the rights of others. [Star Theaters] does not tolerate discrimination or harassment of any kind because these actions clearly infringe on the rights of others.

[Star Theaters] is committed to providing a workplace free from discrimination or harassment based on a person's sex, age, ethnicity, race, religion, or any other legally protected characteristic. Any obvious or implied discrimination is not allowed. Violators of this policy will be disciplined, and possibly terminated.

If you witness or are the victim of a single act of discrimination or harassment, please report the incident to your supervisor. Or, if this is inappropriate, please contact [John Carlson]. Any report you make will be confidential and without reprisal.

- **Name the protected characteristics.**

- **Provide at least two contact people for incident reporting.**

Path on CD-ROM: Human resources→Policy→Addressing discrimination and harassment→Addressing discrimination and harassment—example 1

Explaining a change in withholding

INTEROFFICE MEMORANDUM

TO: [   ]
FROM: [   ]
DATE: [   ]
SUBJECT: This change is normal

Congratulations on the birth of your baby!

I have received your new withholding form reflecting the change in the number of your dependents. By my calculations, this will [increase/decrease] the federal withholding from your check by [amount] and [increase/decrease] the state withholding by [amount].

If this does not meet with your approval or you have any questions please let me know.

- Respond personally, if appropriate, to the event spurring the change in withholding.

- Show how the change will affect the person's take-home pay.

Path on CD-ROM: Human resources→Benefits→Explaining a change in withholding→Explaining a change in withholding—example 1

Explaining FMLA

INTEROFFICE MEMORANDUM

TO: [   ]
FROM: [   ]
DATE: [   ]
SUBJECT: Family and medical leave

Employers have come a long, long way from the days when children and adults alike worked 14-hour days six days a week. In fact, today's organizations, including [company] have become very "family friendly." Our adherence to the Family and Medical Leave Act is an important aspect of our commitment to employees and their families.

Who is eligible?

Employees who have at least one year of service and have worked a minimum of 1,250 hours during the year before the leave is requested.

What leave is available?

Eligible employees may take up to a total of 12 weeks of unpaid leave per calendar year.

When may FMLA leaves be taken?

These leaves may be taken for the birth of a child, the placement of a child for adoption or foster care, caring for seriously ill family members, or your own serious health condition. Leave must be taken for more than a week to be counted as FMLA leave.

How far in advance must the leave be requested?

When a leave is foreseeable, the request must be made 30 days in advance. When the need for an FMLA leave is unexpected, the request must be made as soon as possible.

More details about taking leave under FMLA are covered in the employee handbook. If you have any questions, please see me.

- **Be sure to check and write about all the rules applicable to your company at the time you write.**

- **Use a format, such as Q&A that aids employees' reading and understanding.**

Path on CD-ROM: Human resources→Legal→Explaining FMLA at company→Explaining FMLA at company—example 1

General release

[DATE]

[Name]
[Address]
[City, State ZIP]

Dear [   ]:

Welcome to [company]. We are pleased to have you aboard.

In addition to the other standard paperwork new employees must fill out and return, [company] asks all employees to sign a general release that releases and indemnifies the company from any claims or causes of action they might file. Please read the enclosed document carefully. We encourage you to have a lawyer review it before you sign it.

If you have any questions, please let me know.

Sincerely,

[Name]
[Title]

- Explain the general nature of the release.

- Encourage the employee to take time to read, and possibly have a lawyer review, the release.

Path on CD-ROM: Human resources→Legal→Asking new employee to sign general release→Asking new employee to sign general release—example 1

Offering an entry-level position

[DATE]

[Name]
[Title]
[Company]
[Address]
[City, State ZIP]

Dear [   ]:

It's my pleasure to offer you the position of editorial assistant with a starting salary of [$20,000] a year. Please plan to start on [March 2], and let me know right away if you cannot start on that date.

As we discussed, the position requires some travel to cover trade shows relevant to the magazines you'll be working on. Whenever possible, you will be advised at least 30 days in advance of these required trips.

Your first 90 days here will be considered an orientation period. During this time, [Affinity Magazines] takes special care to make sure we have all made the right decision. You'll meet twice with your supervisor (once at 30 days, again at 60 days) and we'll provide orientation and training to help you learn the ropes.

[Betty] from human resources will soon be sending you a training schedule and other materials relevant to your starting.

Please confirm your acceptance of our offer. If you have any questions, [Betty] or I will be glad to help. We look forward to hearing from you—and to seeing you on [March 2]. We believe this marks the start of an outstanding career.

Sincerely,

[Name]
[Title]

- **Cover major details such as salary, start date and orientation expectations.**

- **Request confirmation of acceptance.**

Path on CD-ROM: Human resources→Hiring→Offering entry-level position→Offering entry-level position—example 1

Praising a temp

[DATE]

[Name/Title]
[Business/Organization Name]
[Address]
[City, State ZIP]

Dear [   ]:

Many thanks for the loan of [*name*] during our recent staff shortage. It is easy to see why you consider her your right-hand person, and we are surprised you were able to function without her for the past three weeks.

If ever anyone had an intuitive sense for spotting office problems before they occur, it must be [*name*]. She headed off several potential crises, both major and minor, and finally helped us fix the photocopier that had been giving us so many problems. Even [*name*], our copier repairman, was pleasantly surprised.

We appreciate your generosity and return [*name*] to you with our most sincere appreciation, and the utmost regret that you are a good enough friend to lend her to us in the first place. If you were not, we would steal her in a heartbeat.

Thanks again, [*name*].

Warm regards,

[Name]
[Title]

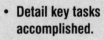

- **Detail key tasks accomplished.**

- **Offer thanks and express appreciation for positive working relationship.**

Path on CD-ROM: Human resources→Temp→Praise→Praise—example 1

Providing a life insurance conversion form

[DATE]

[Name]
[Address]
[City, State ZIP]

Dear [   ]:

In response to your inquiry, I am providing you with the necessary form, "Conversion of Group Life Benefits to a Personal Policy."

For further assistance, you may contact the [insurance company] office nearest you. Call [800 number] or use the phone book to find the most convenient location.

If you have questions, please let me know.

Sincerely,

[Name]
[Title]

- **Note that your letter responds to an inquiry.**

- **Suggest ways for the person to get more information.**

Path on CD-ROM: Human resources→Benefits→Providing life insurance conversion form→Providing life insurance conversion form—example 1

Rejecting a candidate

[DATE]

[Name]
[Title]
[Company]
[Address]
[City, State ZIP]

Dear [   ]:

Thanks for your interest in working for the [Association of Speed Typists]. We enjoyed meeting with you and were impressed to hear about your work on the [membership campaign for the HB Association].

We want to assure you that it was a difficult decision. The pool of candidates was highly qualified. At this point, we have offered the position to another person who is scheduled to start next month.

I know you would also have done a great job for the [Association]. Thanks again for coming in. I wish you the best.

Sincerely,

[Name]
[Title]

• **Find something specific from the candidate's resume or interview to compliment.**

• **Personalize the closing as much as possible.**

Path on CD-ROM: Human resources→Hiring→Rejecting after interview→Rejecting after interview—example 1

Reminder to employees

INTEROFFICE MEMORANDUM

TO: [   ]
FROM: [   ]
DATE: [   ]
SUBJECT: [Be on time]

In the case of being on time to work, good things don't come to those who wait. Employees who wait to come in until after starting time—or don't come in at all—hurt themselves and the company. Tardy or absent employees jeopardize their ability to do good work, to strengthen relationships with their colleagues and supervisors, and to receive rewards for their efforts.

Of course, [A2Z Widgets] suffers a loss in productivity when employees are late or absent. Because of this, the company policy requests that employees let their supervisors know as soon as possible of an unplanned, necessary change in work schedule. The policy also outlines disciplinary action, including termination, for regularly tardy and absent employees.

If you're one of those employees challenged to come in on time or to come in at all, don't wait to change your habits. Come on time every day. You and your company will both reap the benefits.

- **Outline acceptable behavior and the consequences of unacceptable behavior.**

- **Invite employees to do better.**

Path on CD-ROM: Human resources→Employee relations→Reminding employees to be on time→Reminding employees to be on time—example 1

Requesting continuing professional development

INTEROFFICE MEMORANDUM

TO: [   ]
FROM: [   ]
DATE: [   ]
SUBJECT: [Request for professional development authorization]

Learning is a lifelong process. While we all learn every day at work, sometimes it's important to get the kind of structured, traditional learning that a professional development seminar offers.

A seminar on [advanced spreadsheet design] is being offered through the university extension next month. [Verity Financial] would benefit in several ways by sending me to this program.

First, increasing my knowledge of [advanced spreadsheet functions] would enhance my contributions to the [current spreadsheet redesign project]. Second, supporting my attendance would enhance our employer-employee relationship. In addition, I will be able to share what I have learned with other employees upon my return.

The course costs [$180] for a [one-day session], which really is very little money for so many benefits. The class meets [Sept. 2], a relatively slow day in the [accounting department].

Please don't hesitate to contact me with questions. Thank you for considering my request.

- **Emphasize how the company will benefit from granting your request.**

- **Show how the cost of the program is far outweighed by the benefits.**

Path on CD-ROM: Human resources→Employee request→Requesting continuing professional development→Requesting continuing professional development—example 1

Requesting vacation time

INTEROFFICE MEMORANDUM

TO: [   ]
FROM: [   ]
DATE: [   ]
SUBJECT: [Vacation request]

Some of my best business ideas come to me when I'm not at work. That's why vacations, while always tough to schedule into the workload, are so important.

I'd like to plan to be out of the office from [Sept. 5 to Sept. 10]. This would use [five days] of vacation time. As you know, I will leave all my current projects up to date and make [Rosie] aware of their status.

Please let me know as soon as you can if this would be all right, so I can finalize the necessary travel arrangements.

Thank you.

- **Assure your supervisor that you will have your work in good order when you leave.**

- **Be specific about which dates you would like to be away and how much vacation time you will be using.**

Path on CD-ROM: Human resources→Employee request→Requesting vacation time→Requesting vacation time—example 1

Training as a reward

[DATE]

[Name/Title]
[Business/Organization Name]
[Address]
[City, State ZIP]

Dear [   ]:

Many are called but few are chosen, as the saying goes. We are happy to inform you that you were one of those chosen by our judging panel, and that your annual report has been selected to receive a [first place Gold Award] in our marketing competition. Congratulations!

All [first-place winners] will be publicly announced at [the upcoming Leadership Symposium] scheduled for [April 12-15] at [Kiawah Island Resort]. We are keeping it a secret until then. But we hope you will be able to attend the symposium and enjoy the recognition and honor you deserve for your outstanding work.

We have attached registration materials, and planned a special luncheon to announce all winning attendees. We look forward to seeing you there.

Again, congratulations on your [Gold Award]! It is an achievement of which you and your staff can be very proud.

Best regards,

[Name]
[Title]

- **Explain what the person is being recognized for.**

- **Detail the plans for the symposium.**

Path on CD-ROM: Human resources→Training→Employee→Employee—example 1

Accounting and Finance

Chapter 7

Letters written about accounting or other financial matters generally deliver negative news in a straightforward manner. Since the letter represents a contact with a customer, they should show your company in a positive way even when the news is negative.

Key points to remember when writing letters about a customer's overdue account:

- If the news you are delivering is bad, use a positive or neutral buffer. However, do not use a buffer if you think that the reader will not read the whole message.
- State the pertinent information about the customer's account.
- Explain what you want the customer to do about the account.
- Ask the customer to pay the account.
- In later collection letters, tell the customer the consequences of not paying the account.
- Do not threaten legal action unless you are prepared to take it.
- Stress that it is the customer's responsibility for paying the amount owed.
- State your willingness to work with the customer to clear up the overdue account.
- End on a future-looking statement.

Collections

When writing collections letters, just remember the general advice given at the beginning of this chapter.

COLLECTIONS

During the holidays

[DATE]

[Name]
[Address]
[City, State ZIP]

Dear [   ]:

[Ibson Corporation] offers sincere good wishes for the holiday season. We hope your sales exceed those of the previous year.

We realize this is a busy time of the year, but we're anxious to have our receivables up-to-date before the end of the year. Currently you owe [$11,988] on your account.

Since your account is now [60 days past due], would you take a few minutes to send us your payment?

Your cooperation is greatly appreciated.

Sincerely,

[Name]
[Title]

- **Encourages the customer to take care of the overdue amount by the end of the year.**

- **Adding the holiday wishes conveys the idea that the company cares about the customer.**

Path on CD-ROM: Accounting/Finance→Collections→Holiday→Holiday—example 1

Explanation promising payment

[DATE]

[Name/Title]
[Business/Organization Name]
[Address]
[City, State ZIP]

Dear [   ]:

We have received your recent inquiry and are fully aware that we are sixty days in arrears. We appreciate your patience and your willingness to help us resolve this situation.

The current economy has had a negative effect on business growth. That, along with some short-term notes coming due, has caused a temporary cash flow crunch for our firm. We look forward to that flow being restored within the next two to three months as the notes are satisfied and some new products enter the market.

Our outstanding invoice totals [$3,760]. Enclosed please find a check for [$1,000] to help satisfy that debt. We anticipate paying you an additional [$1,000] each month for two months, and the balance of [$760] by [mid-July].

Again, we appreciate your patience and flexibility and look forward to our continued relationship.

Sincerely,

[Name]
[Title]

- **Explain what the problem is and ask for understanding.**

- **Offer a partial payment if possible.**

Path on CD-ROM: Accounting/Finance→Collections→Explanation→Explanation—example 1

COLLECTIONS

Requests, first

[DATE]

[Name]
[Company]
[Address]
[City, State ZIP]

Dear [   ]:

We know our customers have many priorities in their lives. Perhaps those priorities have caused you to inadvertently overlook the bill we sent you in [September] for [$47.50].

Because you're a valued customer, I want to encourage you to take care of this matter by sending us your payment now.

Please remit the full amount by [October 15th]. If there is a problem with this, please call and we can work out other payment arrangements.

Sincerely,

[Name]
[Title]

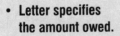

- **Letter specifies the amount owed.**

- **Letter assumes that the customer has just forgotten to pay the bill.**

Path on CD-ROM: Accounting/Finance→Collections→First request→First request—example 1

Requests, second, example #1

[DATE]

[Name]
[Address]
[City, State ZIP]

Dear [   ]:

You may have had a good reason to overlook the first notice we sent you on [October 1] for the [$153] remaining on your account. However, I want to remind you that not paying your bill in a timely fashion can jeopardize your credit rating.

You have been a valued customer for [over 10 years] and I want you to know that we sincerely appreciate your business. Please remit the amount due in the enclosed envelope as soon as possible. If there is a problem and you are unable to pay the bill in full, please call me at [800/555-5555] to arrange a payment schedule.

We look forward to your continued business.

Sincerely,

[Name]
[Title]

- **Customer is treated with sensitivity and honesty.**

- **Customer is notified of the availability of payment options.**

Path on CD-ROM: Accounting/Finance→Collections→Second request→Second request—example 1

Requests, second, example #2

[DATE]

[Name]
[Address]
[City, State ZIP]

Dear [   ]:

We appreciate you choosing [Walbrings] for many of your office supply needs.

This is just a friendly reminder that the [$21.87] you owe us for the paper shredder is now 30 days past due. Enclosed is a postage paid envelope for your convenience. We don't want your status as a valued customer to be jeopardized.

If there is a problem with paying this bill, please call me to arrange an alternative payment plan. And if this letter and your check have crossed in the mail, please accept my apologies for this reminder.

Sincerely,

[Name]
[Title]

- **Letter states how long the bill is overdue.**

- **The postage paid envelope makes it easy for the customer to act.**

Path on CD-ROM: Accounting/Finance→Collections→Second request→Second request—example 2

Requests, third, example #1

[DATE]

[Name]
[Company]
[Address]
[City, State ZIP]

Dear [   ]:

I am at a loss as to why you would want to jeopardize your good credit with us. On [January 15 and February 1] we sent you reminders about your overdue bill. As of today you still have not made payment arrangements for the [$76.99] you owe us.

Please send us the full amount by [March 1] or we will be forced to turn your account over to a collection agency. We would hate to see that happen to one of our valued customers. If there is a situation that we should be made aware of, please call me and we can discuss a more flexible payment schedule.

Sincerely,

[Name]
[Title]

- **Letter emphasizes consequences for nonpayment.**

- **Letter notifies customer of the availability of flexible payment arrangements.**

Path on CD-ROM: Accounting/Finance→Collections→Third request→Third request—example 1

Requests, third, example #2

[DATE]

[Name]
[Address]
[City, State ZIP]

Dear [   ]:

When I reviewed our list of past due accounts yesterday, I was dismayed to see your name still on the past due list.

On [April 24 and May 23] we sent you reminders of the [$675] you owe us for the [lawnmower] you purchased on [February 15]. Frankly, I thought that those reminders would have encouraged you to fulfill your payment obligations.

If you do not remit the [$675] in full by [June 30], we will close your line of credit with our store. And we will add a penalty of [1%] of the full amount for each day of nonpayment after [June 30]. I urge you to take care of this immediately to preserve your good credit history.

If you are unable to pay the full amount, contact me for payment arrangements.

Sincerely,

[Name]
[Title]

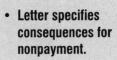

- Letter specifies consequences for nonpayment.

- Letter is courteous, yet firm.

Path on CD-ROM: Accounting/Finance→Collections→Third request→Third request—example 2

Requests, fourth

[DATE]

[Name]
[Address]
[City, State ZIP]

Dear [   ]:

On [March 11], we sent you a pallet of [40 lb. bags of peat moss], which totaled [$395]. According to our credit terms, you agreed to pay the bill within 30 days of receiving the merchandise, which would be [April 10]. Now, 90 days later, and after three reminders, you have made no effort to settle your account or even tell us why you have not done so.

I had hoped that after the third reminder you would pay the bill. We honored your request to deliver the merchandise. Don't you feel a responsibility to honor our request for payment?

If we do not hear from you within 10 days, we will be forced to seek legal recourse.

We can avert a legal solution if you send your check today.

Sincerely,

[Name]
[Title]

- **Remind the customer of the date of the order and the several bills that have been sent.**

- **State the consequences of nonpayment.**

Path on CD-ROM: Accounting/Finance→Collections→Fourth request→Fourth request—example

COLLECTIONS

Requests, last, example #1

[DATE]

[Name]
[Company]
[Address]
[City, State ZIP]

Dear [   ]:

Despite repeated attempts on [June 30 and July 31] to contact you about your overdue bill, you have failed to make satisfactory payment arrangements. Therefore, if we do not hear from you within 72 hours, we will turn your account over to a collection agency.

We very much regret having to take this step. To prevent this from further damaging your credit, please remit the [$137] in full today.

Sincerely,

[Name]
[Title]

- **Letter states the consequences of nonpayment.**

- **Letter reiterates the amount the customer owes.**

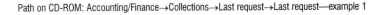

Path on CD-ROM: Accounting/Finance→Collections→Last request→Last request—example 1

Requests, last, example #2

[DATE]

[Name]
[Address]
[City, State ZIP]

Dear [   ]:

Our credit and collections department has notified me of the [$436.51] outstanding on your account. Since [November 14], we have sent you repeated reminders of your overdue bill and as of today have not received a payment, much less a response to our frequent reminders.

As a result, if we don't hear from you within five days, we are turning your account over to a collection agency. Although your past business is appreciated, we cannot let this debt go uncollected any longer.

We hope you will take care of this matter immediately so we can reinstate you in our roster of active clients.

Sincerely,

[Name]
[Title]

- **Letter states that the company wants to keep the customer.**

- **Letter gives a deadline for customer to respond before action is taken.**

Path on CD-ROM: Accounting/Finance→Collections→Last request→Last request—example 2

Streetwise Business Letters

Repossession, example #1

[DATE]

[Name]
[Address]
[City, State ZIP]

Dear [   ]:

We regret that we are forced to repossess the [stove and refrigerator] you purchased from us on [September 13] due to your failure to pay the [$1,539] on your account.

On [December 11], representatives from our company will arrive at your home at [9 a.m.] to collect the [stove and refrigerator].

We had hoped that the flexible credit options we offered would prevent this from happening. But your refusal to contact us and work out a payment schedule has left us no other option.

Sincerely,

[Name]
[Title]

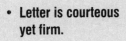

- **Letter is courteous yet firm.**

- **Letter states consequences of nonpayment.**

Path on CD-ROM: Accounting/Finance→Collections→Repossession→Repossession—example 1

Repossession, example #2

[DATE]

[Name]
[Company]
[Address]
[City, State ZIP]

Dear [   ]:

Despite our repeated attempts to work out a flexible payment schedule, [Pyramid Company] has not made a payment on the [$7,987] due on its account. The account is now [120] days past due.

Because of this, we have the right to begin repossession of the [computer equipment] you purchased from us.

Accordingly, representatives from our company will be at [Pyramid Company on May 16 at 10 a.m.] to collect:

[• 3 Pentium CPUs]
[• 3 VGA color monitors]
[• 3 keyboards]
[• 6 training modules including books, software and videos]
[• 3 computer desks]
[• 3 laser printers]

We regret we need to take this extreme action. Your failure to send us a payment left us no other choice.

Sincerely,

[Name]
[Title]

- **Letter states amount owed and how long overdue.**

- **Letter is courteous, yet firm.**

Path on CD-ROM: Accounting/Finance→Collections→Repossession→Repossession—example 2

Credit

Key points to remember when writing credit letters include:

- Use a positive or neutral buffer if the news is negative.
- When you have a reason that readers will understand and respect, give the reason before the negative news.
- Make the negative news clear.
- Offer an alternative or compromise, if appropriate.
- Thank the customer for applying for credit.
- Encourage future business, either using the credit or on a cash basis.
- End with a future-looking statement.

Acknowledgment

[DATE]

[Name]
[Company]
[Address]
[City, State ZIP]

Dear [   ]:

We received your purchase order [#67954 on January 16]. Thank you for considering [Hot 'n Cold Supply for your HVAC] equipment needs.

Before we can extend our normal terms of net 30 days, we will need the following information:

* Name of your bank, account number, and contact
* Names of two suppliers with whom you are currently doing business
* An income statement and balance sheet

[Hot 'n Cold Supply] looks forward to serving you. Thank you for your cooperation and for your order.

Sincerely,

[Name]
[Title]

* Letter specifies what financial data customer needs to provide in order for company to make a decision.

* Cordial tone welcomes the customer.

Path on CD-ROM: Accounting/Finance→Credit→Acknowledgment→Acknowledgment—example 1

Approval

[DATE]

[Name/Title]
[Business/Organization Name]
[Address]
[City, State ZIP]

Dear [   ]:

In today's uncertain economy, there simply are too many risks.

That goes for our customers, too. We selectively choose those with whom we prefer to do business and those to whom we extend credit. It is a precautionary measure that helps keep service costs down, allowing us to offer the most competitive rates possible to those we serve.

After a close review of your credit history, we are pleased to offer your company a full line of credit toward purchases made from our business. Please fill out the attached application, which will allow us to set up your account.

Welcome to our customer family. We look forward to doing more business with you.

Sincerely,

[Name]
[Title]

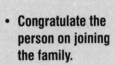

- **Congratulate the person on joining the family.**

- **Explain the next steps in the process.**

Path on CD-ROM: Accounting/Finance→Credit→Approving→Approving—example 1

Canceling

[DATE]

[Name]
[Company]
[Address]
[City, State ZIP]

Dear [   ]:

After a review of our accounts, we find that you are still [$3,679] in arrears. Although you are a valued customer of [Krall Hardware] and have made several attempts to reduce the amount you owe us, you also have continued to charge merchandise.

Because of this, we are canceling your credit privileges. The balance of [$3,679] is now due in full. Please contact me to make payment arrangements.

You may reapply for reinstatement of credit privileges once you have taken care of this matter.

Sincerely,

[Name]
[Title]

- **Explain that the customer's credit has been canceled.**

- **Explain the reason for canceling customer's credit.**

Path on CD-ROM: Accounting/Finance→Credit→Cancel credit→Cancel credit—example 1

CREDIT

Inquiry

[DATE]

[Name]
[Address]
[City, State ZIP]

Dear [   ]:

A purchase order from [Parties 'R Us, 948 N. Main St., Centerville, NY] for [$75] worth of merchandise listed you as a credit reference.

We would appreciate any information you can provide on the credit history of [Parties 'R Us] with your company. Key facts would include how long the owner, [Donna Gard], has had an account with you and whether or not she has any outstanding debts. We will keep any information you send us confidential.

I've enclosed a postage paid envelope for your convenience.

Sincerely,

[Name]
[Title]

- **Letter assures recipient of confidentiality.**

- **Letter requests specific information on applicant's financial status.**

Path on CD-ROM: Accounting/Finance→Credit→Inquiry→Inquiry—example 1

Reference

[DATE]

[Name]
[Company]
[Address]
[City, State ZIP]

Dear [   ]:

This correspondence is in response to your letter of [April 23] requesting credit information on [Parties 'R Us]. Owner [Donna Gard] has placed orders totaling [$500] with us over the past [six months]. She has paid her bills in full within 30 days of shipping the products.

On the basis of our experience with her, we believe [Ms. Gard] to be credit worthy.

Sincerely,

[Name]
[Title]

- **Response states how long the account was open, amounts owed and the record of payment.**

- **Clearly define your conclusion.**

CREDIT

Refusal

[DATE]

[Name]
[Address]
[City, State ZIP]

Dear [   ]:

Thank you for applying for the [Ultra gasoline card]. Our credit department has carefully reviewed your application.

Based on the financial information you reported, your debt to income ratio is greater than the percentage we can allow our applicants to have. Therefore we must unfortunately deny you a card at this time.

Thank you again for your interest in the [Ultra gasoline card]. We hope we can approve an application of yours at a future date.

Sincerely,

[Name]
[Title]

- **Letter gives reason for the denial**

- **Letter encourages customer to reapply at a later date.**

Path on CD-ROM: Accounting/Finance→Credit→Refusal→Refusal—example 1

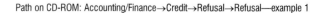

Restrictions

[DATE]

[Name]
[Company]
[City, State ZIP]

Dear [   ]:

After [18 months] of prompt payments, we've noticed that your last [two bills were 30 days late]. We are concerned about the change in your payment pattern. Rather than cancel your credit line, we have reduced it 50%.

If, after six months, you are current with your bills, we will reevaluate an increase in your credit line.

Your business is important to us. We hope we can increase your credit line in the future.

Sincerely,

[Name]
[Title]

- **Letter explains reasons for restrictions.**

- **Letter states when the account will be reviewed.**

Path on CD-ROM: Accounting/Finance→Credit→Restrictions→Restrictions—example 1

Purchasing

The by-words of an effective purchasing manager are "care" and "concern"— care that all significant details are identified and communicated precisely, and concern that solid relationships with all suppliers are maintained. During the early bidding and negotiation processes and later as contracts are being reviewed and approved or rejected, purchasing managers communicate a wide variety of messages. They encourage new bidders, negotiate revisions, point out problems regarding compliance to contracts, and convey both acceptances and rejections.

To guarantee an effective purchasing process in general, follow these recommendations:

- Explain how you heard about the vendor's products or services.
- Specify only the products or services you want. Consider explaining what you do not want as well.
- Be as precise as possible about times, deadlines, and project specifications.
- Express appreciation for the effort involved in developing the proposal.
- Treat each bid and contract as facets of an ongoing vendor partnership.

Accepting a bid

[DATE]

[Name]
[Company]
[Address]
[City, State ZIP]

Dear [   ]:

Your bid for a series of [computer training] seminars for our [front-line] staff closely fits our goals in employee professional development. We have accepted your proposal and are looking forward to putting your plan into action soon.

We especially appreciated the small class sizes and your ability to schedule classes early in the mornings and late in the afternoons.

We will send a contract to you by [August 10] and look forward to working with you in the months ahead.

Sincerely,

[Name]
[Title]

- **The good news is up front, in the first paragraph.**

- **Letter mentions key reasons that the company selected this particular proposal.**

Path on CD-ROM: Purchasing→Bidding-negotiations→Acceptance→Acceptance—example 1

PURCHASING

Addressing contract changes

[Name]
[Company]
[Address]
[City, State ZIP]

Dear [   ]:

Yesterday we received your signed contract for [replacement of the shingles on the roof of our antiques shop]. We noted the changes you made, particularly the change in [color from dark green to red shingles]. Since you have [red shingles] in your current inventory, the use of [red shingles would decrease our cost by 15 percent].

We originally selected [dark green shingles to harmonize with the building's exterior and the adjacent buildings in this rejuvenated, turn-of-the-century business district]. Although we appreciate your efforts to lower our [roof replacement costs, we do not want the red shingles].

We cannot initial this contract change. We will stick with [the dark green shingles and pay the additional cost].

Thank you for your attention to this important aspect of our contract. Please call if you have any questions about [this roofing project].

We hope to see your crew here as planned on the 15th and are looking forward to our new, green roof.

Cordially,

[Name]
[Title]

- **First paragraph serves to buffer the rejection of proposed changes.**

- **Rejection is stated directly and clearly.**

Path on CD-ROM: Purchasing→Contracts→Changes altered→Changes altered—example 1

Compliment to vendor

[DATE]

[Name]
[Company]
[Address]
[City, State ZIP]

Dear [   ]:

Thank you for your quick response last week in repairing our office building. When the storm tore half of the roof off, I expected that fixing the problem would take weeks. Despite heavy damage to many other buildings in the area, [name] and your other crew members were on the scene the very next day.

The completed job looks great. I cannot see where the old roof ends and the new one begins.

Thank you for a job well done.

Sincerely,

[Name]
[Title]

- Specify exactly what you like about the product or service.

- Identify the employees responsible for your satisfaction.

Path on CD-ROM: Purchasing→Shipping-Delivery→Compliment to vendor→Compliment to vendor—example 1

PURCHASING

Contract billing error

[DATE]

[Name]
[Company]
[Address]
[City, State ZIP]

Dear [   ]:

Yesterday we received your invoice for [computer training] for our [front-line] staff. It indicates that we owe you for providing [five two-hour training sessions last month, for 12 employees at each session].

Please note that your instructors presented only [four sessions on the 6th, 13th, 20th and 27th of last month to 10 employees on each date]. I am returning your invoice and a copy of our class attendance records, signed by your instructor.

Thank you for your prompt attention to this issue.

Sincerely,

[Name]
[Title]

- **Enclosing relevant documentation can help clear up an error as soon as possible.**

- **Letter explains the error in detail.**

Path on CD-ROM: Purchasing→Contracts→Billing error→Billing error—example 1

Notification of non-compliance

[DATE]

[Name]
[Company]
[Address]
[City, State ZIP]

Dear [   ]:

While we have been pleased at the speed with which your company has been [installing an elevator, ramp and automatic door at our building, we are concerned that this work may not entirely adhere to the standards of our contract].

Our maintenance engineer has noted that the [opening for the automatic door and the level of pitch of the ramp do not meet state administrative codes for accommodations for physically disabled adults. He is also concerned that the door that has arrived on site was not manufactured by the company indicated in our contract.]

To save the expense and time of redoing much of this work, please review the contract specifications and ensure that your crew is following them.

Thank you for your attention to this matter. We are all looking forward to the advantages of a fully accessible building.

Sincerely,

[Name]
[Title]

- **Letter provides specific details of the areas of non-compliance.**

- **Close assumes the problems will be addressed and resolved.**

Path on CD-ROM: Purchasing→Contracts→Notification of non-compliance→Notification of non-compliance—example 1

PURCHASING

Requesting a proposal

[DATE]

[Name]
[Company]
[Address]
[City, State ZIP]

Dear [   ]:

I noticed the column you wrote for a recent issue of [*New Jersey Freight News*] and wanted to let you know that I agree completely with your comments about the [current regulatory climate]. My company is a small but fast-growing [freight carrier, and your column made me realize that it is now large enough to require the services of an accounting firm, especially during tax season]. Of course, we have a [business] office; but the addition of specialized [accounting services] no doubt could help it operate more effectively.

Please send me a proposal for [accounting] services that would include the completion of [all tax forms and regular consulting about our company's compliance with the new regulatory standards]. Since our company has less than [$5 million in revenues], cost is an important consideration in choosing an accounting firm.

I would like to select [an accounting] firm before [fourth quarter], in order to begin working with its professional staff well in advance [of tax season]. I am looking forward to receiving your proposal and learning more about your firm.

Sincerely,

[Name]
[Title]

- **Writer mentions how he learned of the accounting firm.**

- **Letter ends with a request for action.**

Path on CD-ROM: Purchasing→Bidding-negotiations→Making bids and quotes→Making bids and quotes—example 1

Returning item

[DATE]

[Name]
[Company]
[Address]
[City, State ZIP]

Dear [   ]:

Today we received [eight of your company's "Amish-inspired" arm chairs], which we ordered for our conference room. All of them were damaged in transit. [Three have loose legs. One has a leg that has broken off completely. All eight chairs have scratched legs. We are returning them.]

Please send [new chairs] as quickly as possible. [Our board of directors is looking forward to holding their next meeting in our renovated conference room on [date].]

Thank you.

Sincerely,

[Name]
[Title]

- **Assess and describe the problems.**

- **State any time demands; the vendor's best interests lie in satisfying you as his customer.**

Path on CD-ROM: Purchasing→Shipping-delivery→Returning item→Returning item—example 4

Vendor contact information

[DATE]

[Name]
[Company]
[Address]
[City, State ZIP]

Dear [   ]:

We are updating our vendor records. To make it easier for our purchasing agents to contact you, please review the attached page, so that we have the correct telephone number, mailing address and account representatives listed for your firm.

Please also provide your e-mail address and Web site, if available, and indicate whether you accept on-line orders.

Thank you for your assistance in ensuring that our transactions are as smooth as possible.

Sincerely,

[Name]
[Title]

- Letter explains the request and the reason for it as succinctly as possible.

- Request is you-centered, pointing out to the vendor the benefit of replying.

Path on CD-ROM: Purchasing→Contracts→Vendor request→Vendor request—example 1

Developed by Adams Media, **BusinessTown.com** is a free informational site for entrepreneurs, small business owners, and operators. It provides a comprehensive guide for planning, starting, growing, and managing a small business.

Visitors may access hundreds of articles addressing dozens of business topics, participate in forums as well as connect to additional resources around the Web. **BusinessTown.com** is easily navigated and provides assistance to small businesses and start-ups. The material covers beginning basic issues as well as the more advanced topics.

✓ **Accounting**
Basic, Credit & Collections, Projections, Purchasing/Cost Control

✓ **Advertising**
Magazine, Newspaper, Radio, Television, Yellow Pages

✓ **Business Opportunities**
Ideas for New Businesses, Business for Sale, Franchises

✓ **Business Plans**
Creating Plans & Business Strategies

✓ **Finance**
Getting Money, Money Problem Solutions

✓ **Letters & Forms**
Looking Professional, Sample Letters & Forms

✓ **Getting Started**
Incorporating, Choosing a Legal Structure

✓ **Hiring & Firing**
Finding the Right People, Legal Issues

✓ **Home Business**
Home Business Ideas, Getting Started

✓ **Internet**
Getting Online, Put Your Catalog on the Web

✓ **Legal Issues**
Contracts, Copyrights, Patents, Trademarks

✓ **Managing a Small Business**
Growth, Boosting Profits, Mistakes to Avoid, Competing with the Giants

✓ **Managing People**
Communications, Compensation, Motivation, Reviews, Problem Employees

✓ **Marketing**
Direct Mail, Marketing Plans, Strategies, Publicity, Trade Shows

✓ **Office Setup**
Leasing, Equipment, Supplies

✓ **Presentations**
Know Your Audience, Good Impression

✓ **Sales**
Face to Face, Independent Reps, Telemarketing

✓ **Selling a Business**
Finding Buyers, Setting a Price, Legal Issues

✓ **Taxes**
Employee, Income, Sales, Property, Use

✓ **Time Management**
Can you Really Manage Time?

✓ **Travel & Maps**
Making Business Travel Fun

✓ **Valuing a Business**
Simple Valuation Guidelines

STREETWISE® BOOKS

New for Fall 2002!

**Complete Business Plan
with Software**
$29.95
ISBN 1-58062-798-6

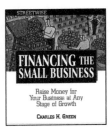

Financing the Small Business
$19.95
ISBN 1-58062-765-X

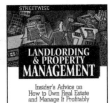

**Landlording & Property
Management**
$19.95
ISBN 1-58062-766-8

Project Management
$19.95
ISBN 1-58062-770-6

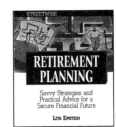

Retirement Planning
$19.95
ISBN 1-58062-772-2

Also Available in the Streetwise Series:

24 Hour MBA
$19.95
ISBN 1-58062-256-9

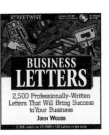

**Achieving Wealth
Through Franchising**
$19.95
ISBN 1-58062-503-7

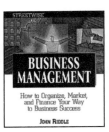

**Business Letters
w/CD-ROM**
$24.95
ISBN 1-58062-133-3

Business Management
$19.95
ISBN 1-58062-540-1

Complete Business Plan
$19.95
ISBN 1-55850-845-7

**Customer-Focused
Selling**
$19.95
ISBN 1-55850-725-6

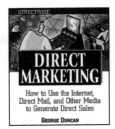

Direct Marketing
$19.95
ISBN 1-58062-439-1

**Do-It-Yourself
Advertising**
$19.95
ISBN 1-55850-727-2

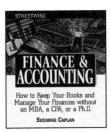

Finance & Accounting
$17.95
ISBN 1-58062-196-1

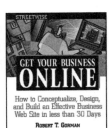

Get Your Business Online
$19.95
ISBN 1-58062-368-9

Adams Streetwise® books for growing your business

Hiring Top Performers
$17.95
ISBN 1-55850-684-5

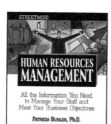

Human Resources Management
$19.95
ISBN 1-58062-699-8

Independent Consulting
$19.95
ISBN 1-55850-728-0

Internet Business Plan
$19.95
ISBN 1-58062-502-9

Low-Cost Web Site Promotion
$19.95
ISBN 1-58062-501-0

Managing a Nonprofit
$19.95
ISBN 1-58062-698-X

Managing People
$19.95
ISBN 1-55850-726-4

Marketing Plan
$17.95
ISBN 1-58062-268-2

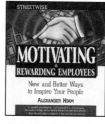

Maximize Web Site Traffic
$19.95
ISBN 1-58062-369-7

Motivating & Rewarding Employees
$17.95
ISBN 1-58062-130-9

Relationship Marketing on the Internet
$17.95
ISBN 1-58062-255-0

Sales Letters w/CD-ROM
$24.95
ISBN 1-58062-440-5

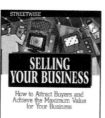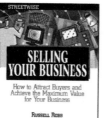

Selling Your Business
$19.95
ISBN 1-58062-602-5

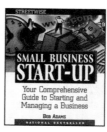

Small Business Start-Up
$17.95
ISBN 1-55850-581-4

Small Business Success Kit w/CD-ROM
$24.95
ISBN 1-58062-367-0

Time Management
$17.95
ISBN 1-58062-131-7

Start Your Own Business Workbook
$9.95
ISBN 1-58062-506-1

Take Your Business Online Workbook
$9.95
ISBN 1-58062-507-X

Available wherever books are sold.
**For more information, or to order,
call 800-872-5627
or visit adamsmedia.com**
Adams Media Corporation
57 Littlefield Street, Avon, MA 02322

Instructions for CD-ROM

Adams Streetwise® Business Letters

Adams Streetwise® Business Letters was designed to serve as a comprehensive business resource, providing you with the letters you need to run your business in the real world.

These letters will help you to manage your finances, close sales, track employee performance, and much, much more. Compatible with all major word processors, this program enables you to quickly develop letters to use as a standard across your organization.

If you want to find one of the letters from the book on the enclosed CD-ROM, simply insert the disk, click on Open a Master Document and follow the steps outlined at the bottom of the letter you have chosen.

SYSTEM REQUIREMENTS
Minimum Requirements
486 PC compatible or higher
Windows 95/98 or NT
2X CD-ROM
8MB of RAM
5MB of free hard drive space

Recommended
486 PC compatible or higher
Windows 95/98 or NT
6X CD-ROM or faster
16MB of RAM or more
20MB of free hard drive space

Installation
Windows 95, 98, & NT

Place disk in CD-ROM drive and close the drive door. Most CD-ROMs will auto-run the installation after the drive door closes.

IF YOUR CD-ROM DOES NOT AUTO-RUN, FOLLOW THE SIMPLE PROCEDURES BELOW.

1) From the Start Menu choose Run.
2) When the Run Window appears, **click** on the Browse button on your right.
3) From the drop down menu, select your CD-ROM drive.
4) Double-click on the file titled "Setup."
5) When the Run Window reappears, Click the Ok button.

By accepting the defaults, the program should install successfully.

TROUBLE SHOOTING

ALWAYS BE SURE THE CD IS IN THE DRIVE

Note that these forms contain a large amount of information in comparison to most items that you print. Occasionally, this may cause a print buffer error on some printers.

To fix, try following these steps.

1) Go to your My Computer icon and double-click.
2) Double-click on the Printer icon.
3) Highlight the printer you are using and go under the File menu and choose Properties.
4) Click on the Details Tab.
5) Hit the button for Spool Settings.
6) Write down you current setting for spool data format.
7) Check off Print directly to Printer.
8) Close all the dialog boxes you have opened and re-start our program.

If you try printing now, it should work, though it may be slow.

To restore your former printer settings, follow the steps above, but choose Spool printer jobs so printing finishes faster and restore your spool data format to what you wrote down above.

The procedure above should fix this problem on most printers. If not please contact technical support.

NOTE:
Updating your printer drivers may also correct your problem. Most major manufacturers have their drivers available for download directly from their website.

How to Reach Us
By Mail: Adams Media Corporation
57 Littlefield Street
Avon, MA 02322.
By phone: (508) 427-7100 x6769
By Fax: (508) 427-6790
By email: techsupport@adamsmedia.com

Technical Support hours are Monday through Friday, between 9 AM and 5 PM, Eastern Time. Before calling, please make sure your computer is turned on, with Adams Streetwise program running and on the screen. When you reach an Adams Media technical support specialist, be prepared to give the following information:

1) The version of Adams Streetwise program (Located in the Help>About section of the program)
2) The type of computer you are using (486, Pentium, model, etc.)
3) The operating system software you are using (Windows 95, 98, Windows NT)

Please note that, when technical support is extremely busy, you may reach voice mail. We have implemented this system to insure you are not paying long distance charges while you are on hold. Please leave a message and someone will get back to you.

Under copyright law, no person shall duplicate, photocopy, reproduce or resell Adams Media software or documentation without the prior written consent of Adams Media Corporation.